# Campbell's ®

## M'm! M'm!
# HOMEMADE
# IN MINUTES

# Campbell's

# M'm! M'm! HOMEMADE IN MINUTES

# POULTRY IN NO TIME

## Asian Chicken Stir-Fry

**Prep Time:** 5 minutes    **Cook Time:** 20 minutes

- 1 tablespoon vegetable oil
- 1 pound skinless, boneless chicken breasts, cut into strips
- 1 can (10¾ ounces) CAMPBELL'S Condensed Golden Mushroom Soup
- 3 tablespoons soy sauce
- 1 teaspoon garlic powder
- 1 bag (16 ounces) frozen vegetable combination, thawed
- 4 cups hot cooked rice

1. In medium skillet over medium-high heat, heat oil. Add chicken and stir-fry until browned and juices evaporate.

2. Add soup, soy sauce and garlic powder. Heat to a boil. Add vegetables and cook over medium heat until vegetables are tender-crisp, stirring often. Serve over rice.         *Serves 4*

*Asian Chicken Stir-Fry*

# Chicken Quesadillas

**Prep Time:** 5 minutes     **Cook Time:** 15 minutes

**1 pound skinless, boneless chicken breasts, cubed**
**1 can (10¾ ounces) CAMPBELL'S Condensed Cheddar Cheese Soup**
**½ cup PACE Thick & Chunky Salsa *or* Picante Sauce (medium)**
**10 flour tortillas (8-inch)**

**1.** Preheat oven to 425°F.

**2.** In medium nonstick skillet over medium-high heat, cook chicken 5 minutes or until no longer pink and juices evaporate, stirring often. Add soup and salsa. Heat through, stirring occasionally.

**3.** Place tortillas on 2 baking sheets. Top ***half*** of each tortilla with ***about ⅓ cup*** soup mixture. Spread to within ½ inch of edge. Moisten edges of tortilla with water. Fold over and seal edges together.

**4.** Bake 5 minutes or until hot.                    *Serves 4*

**Tip:** Serve with Fiesta Rice (page 79).

**timesaver tip**

Substitute 2 cans (5 ounces ***each***) SWANSON Premium Chunk Chicken Breast, drained, for fresh chicken. In step 2 in medium saucepan mix soup, salsa and chicken. Over medium heat, heat through, stirring often. Proceed as in step 3.

*Chicken Quesadillas with Fiesta Rice*

# Easy Chicken & Pasta

**Prep Time:** 5 minutes     **Cook Time:** 25 minutes

> 1 tablespoon vegetable oil
> 1 pound skinless, boneless chicken breasts, cut up
> 1 can (10¾ ounces) CAMPBELL'S Condensed Cream of Mushroom Soup *or* 98% Fat Free Cream of Mushroom Soup
> 2¼ cups water
> ½ teaspoon dried basil leaves, crushed
> 2 cups frozen vegetable combination (broccoli, cauliflower, carrots)
> 2 cups *uncooked* corkscrew macaroni
> Grated Parmesan cheese

**1.** In medium skillet over medium-high heat, heat oil. Add chicken and cook until browned, stirring often. Set chicken aside.

**2.** Add soup, water, basil and vegetables. Heat to a boil. Add *uncooked* macaroni. Reduce heat to medium. Cook 10 minutes, stirring often.

**3.** Return chicken to pan. Cook 5 minutes more or until macaroni is done, stirring often. ***Sprinkle with cheese.***          *Serves 4*

### Your Choice Chicken & Pasta:

| Choose a soup... | Choose a pasta... | Choose a combo... |
| --- | --- | --- |
| CAMPBELL'S Condensed Cream of Chicken Soup *or* 98% Fat Free Cream of Chicken Soup | Uncooked medium tube-shaped macaroni | Broccoli, corn and red peppers combination |
| CAMPBELL'S Condensed Cheddar Cheese Soup | Uncooked spaghetti, broken in half* | Stir-fry *or* Oriental vegetables, no sauce added |
| CAMPBELL'S Condensed Cream of Celery Soup *or* 98% Fat Free Cream of Celery Soup | Uncooked bow tie pasta | Peas and carrots |

*Increase water to 2½ cups. 8 ounces uncooked spaghetti = 2 cups.*

*Easy Chicken & Pasta*

ipe for   Easy Chicken : Pasta
n         Grandma)
ts & Directions      1 TBL VEGETABLE OIL
          SKINLESS, BONELESS CHICKEN BREAST
          CAMPBELL'S CREAM OF MUSHR
          WATER
          DRIED BASI

# Quick Chicken Parmigiana

**Prep Time:** 5 minutes     **Cook Time:** 15 minutes

1 package (about 10 ounces) frozen fully cooked
breaded chicken patties *or* 1 package (about
14 ounces) refrigerated fully cooked breaded
chicken cutlets
1 jar (28 ounces) PREGO Traditional Pasta Sauce
2 tablespoons grated Parmesan cheese
½ cup shredded mozzarella cheese (2 ounces)
4 cups hot cooked spaghetti (about 8 ounces
uncooked)

**1.** In 2-quart shallow baking dish arrange patties. Top each with
¼ *cup* pasta sauce. Sprinkle with Parmesan cheese and
mozzarella cheese.

**2.** Bake at 400°F. for 15 minutes or until chicken is hot and cheese
is melted.

**3.** Heat remaining sauce until hot. Serve sauce with chicken and
spaghetti.                                                                 *Serves 4*

**Time Saver:** In 2-quart shallow microwave-safe baking dish arrange
patties. Microwave on HIGH 4 minutes (3 minutes for refrigerated
cutlets). Top each patty with ¼ *cup* pasta sauce, **1 teaspoon**
Parmesan cheese and **2 tablespoons** mozzarella cheese. Microwave
2 minutes more or until sauce is hot and cheese is melted.

**Chicken Nuggets Parmigiana:** Substitute 1 package (10 to
13 ounces) frozen **or** refrigerated fully cooked breaded chicken
nuggets for chicken patties. In 2-quart shallow microwave-safe
baking dish arrange nuggets. Microwave on HIGH 3½ minutes
(2½ minutes for refrigerated). Pour pasta sauce evenly over
nuggets. Top with cheeses. Microwave 2 minutes more or until
sauce is hot and cheese is melted.

*Top to bottom: Mushroom Mozzarella Bruschetta (page 61)
and Quick Chicken Parmigiana*

# Skillet Herb Roasted Chicken

**Prep Time:** 10 minutes     **Cook Time:** 20 minutes

4 skinless, boneless chicken breast halves (about
    1 pound)
¼ teaspoon ground sage
¼ teaspoon dried thyme leaves, crushed
    Vegetable cooking spray
2 cloves garlic, minced
1 can (10¾ ounces) CAMPBELL'S HEALTHY REQUEST
    Condensed Cream of Chicken Soup
½ cup water
4 cups hot cooked rice, cooked without salt

**1.** Sprinkle chicken with sage and thyme.

**2.** Spray medium nonstick skillet with cooking spray and heat over
medium heat 1 minute. Add chicken and cook 15 minutes or
until chicken is browned and no longer pink. Remove and
keep warm.

**3.** Remove pan from heat. Spray with cooking spray. Add garlic
and cook 30 seconds or until lightly browned.

**4.** Add soup and water. Reduce heat to low and heat through.
Serve over chicken with rice.                    *Serves 4*

**Nutritional Values per Serving:** Calories 457, Total Fat 5g, Saturated Fat 2g,
Cholesterol 79mg, Sodium 361mg, Total Carbohydrate 65g, Protein 33g

**Tip:** Serve with **Herb Broth Simmered Rice:** In medium saucepan
over medium-high heat, heat 1 can (16 ounces) CAMPBELL'S
HEALTHY REQUEST Ready to Serve Chicken Broth to a boil. Add
1 cup uncooked regular long-grain white rice and ½ teaspoon
dried thyme leaves, crushed. Reduced heat to low. Cover and cook
25 minutes or until rice is done and most of liquid is absorbed.

*Skillet Herb Roasted Chicken*

# Country Mustard Chicken

**Prep Time:** 5 minutes     **Cook Time:** 20 minutes

**Vegetable cooking spray**
**4 skinless, boneless chicken breast halves**
**1 jar (12 ounces) FRANCO-AMERICAN Slow Roast**
   **Chicken Gravy**
**1 tablespoon country-style Dijon mustard**
**½ teaspoon garlic powder**

1. Spray medium skillet with cooking spray and heat over medium-high heat 1 minute. Add chicken and cook 10 minutes or until browned. Set chicken aside.

2. Add gravy, mustard and garlic powder. Heat to a boil. Return chicken to pan. Reduce heat to low. Cover and cook 5 minutes or until chicken is no longer pink. Serve with noodles if desired. Sprinkle with chopped parsley.               *Serves 4*

# QUICK SIDE DISH Broccoli & Noodles Supreme

**Prep Time:** 5 minutes     **Cook Time:** 20 minutes

**3 cups *uncooked* medium egg noodles**
**2 cups fresh *or* frozen broccoli flowerets**
**1 can (10¾ ounces) CAMPBELL'S Condensed Cream**
   **of Chicken & Broccoli Soup**
**½ cup sour cream**
**⅓ cup grated Parmesan cheese**
**⅛ teaspoon pepper**

In large saucepan prepare noodles according to package directions. Add broccoli for last 5 minutes of cooking time. Drain. In same pan mix soup, sour cream, cheese, pepper and noodle mixture. Over medium heat, heat through, stirring occasionally.               *Serves 5*

Left to right: *Broccoli & Noodles Supreme*
*and Country Mustard Chicken*

# Tomato-Basil Chicken

**Prep Time:** 5 minutes     **Cook Time:** 20 minutes

1 tablespoon vegetable oil
4 skinless, boneless breast halves (about 1 pound)
1 can (10¾ ounces) CAMPBELL'S Condensed Tomato Soup
½ cup milk
2 tablespoons grated Parmesan cheese
½ teaspoon dried basil leaves, crushed
¼ teaspoon garlic powder *or* 2 cloves garlic, minced
4 cups hot cooked medium tube-shaped macaroni (about 3 cups uncooked)

**1.** In medium skillet over medium-high heat, heat oil. Add chicken and cook 10 minutes or until browned. Set chicken aside. Pour off fat.

**2.** Add soup, milk, cheese, basil and garlic powder. Heat to a boil. Return chicken to pan. Reduce heat to low. Cover and cook 5 minutes or until chicken is no longer pink. Serve with macaroni.

*Serves 4*

**tip**

Cook pasta as chicken is browning. For extra flavor, simmer pasta in broth (see Simple Seasoned Pasta, page 22).

Top to bottom: *Honey-Mustard Chicken (page 24) and Tomato-Basil Chicken*

# Crunchy No-Fry Chicken

**Prep Time:** 10 minutes     **Cook Time:** 20 minutes

¾ cup finely crushed corn flakes
½ teaspoon garlic powder
⅛ teaspoon black pepper
⅛ teaspoon ground red pepper
4 skinless, boneless chicken breast halves
¼ cup SWANSON Chicken Broth

**1.** Mix corn flakes, garlic powder, black pepper and red pepper. Dip chicken into broth. Coat with corn flake mixture.

**2.** Place chicken on baking sheet. Bake at 400°F. for 20 minutes or until chicken is no longer pink.                    *Serves 4*

## QUICK SIDE DISH Glazed Snow Peas & Carrots

**Prep Time:** 15 minutes     **Cook Time:** 10 minutes

4 teaspoons cornstarch
1 can (14½ ounces) SWANSON Vegetable Broth
4 medium carrots, sliced (about 2 cups)
1 medium onion, chopped (about ½ cup)
¾ pound snow peas (about 4 cups)
1 teaspoon lemon juice

**1.** In cup mix cornstarch and *1 cup* broth until smooth. Set aside.

**2.** In medium skillet over high heat, heat remaining broth to a boil. Add carrots and onion. Reduce heat to medium. Cover and cook 5 minutes or until carrots are tender-crisp. Add snow peas. Cook 2 minutes.

**3.** Stir cornstarch mixture and add. Cook until mixture boils and thickens, stirring constantly. Stir in lemon juice.          *Serves 8*

Left to right: *Crunchy No-Fry Chicken, Glazed Snow Peas & Carrots and Garlic Mashed Potatoes (page 77)*

# Lemon Broccoli Chicken

**Prep Time:** 5 minutes    **Cook Time:** 20 minutes

> 1 lemon
> 1 tablespoon vegetable oil
> 4 skinless, boneless chicken breast halves (about 1 pound)
> 1 can (10¾ ounces) CAMPBELL'S Condensed Cream of Broccoli Soup *or* 98% Fat Free Cream of Broccoli Soup
> ¼ cup milk
> ⅛ teaspoon pepper

**1.** Cut 4 thin slices of lemon and set aside. Squeeze 2 teaspoons juice from remaining lemon and set aside.

**2.** In medium skillet over medium-high heat, heat oil. Add chicken and cook 10 minutes or until browned. Set chicken aside. Pour off fat.

**3.** Add soup, milk, reserved lemon juice and pepper. Heat to a boil. Return chicken to pan. Top with lemon slices. Reduce heat to low. Cover and cook 5 minutes or until chicken is no longer pink.

*Serves 4*

## tip

Looking for a quick and delicious side dish your family will love? Top your favorite cooked pasta shape with PREGO Pasta Sauce, a perfect accompaniment to chicken, pork or meat loaf!

*Lemon Broccoli Chicken*

# 25-Minute Chicken & Noodles

**Prep Time:** 10 minutes      **Cook Time:** 15 minutes

> 1 can (14½ ounces) SWANSON Chicken Broth
>    (1¾ cups)
> ½ teaspoon dried basil leaves, crushed
> ⅛ teaspoon pepper
> 2 cups frozen vegetable combination (broccoli,
>    cauliflower, carrots)
> 2 cups *uncooked* medium egg noodles
> 2 cups cubed cooked chicken

**1.** In medium skillet mix broth, basil, pepper and vegetables. Over medium-high heat, heat to a boil. Reduce heat to medium. Cover and cook 5 minutes.

**2.** Stir in noodles. Cover and cook 5 minutes, stirring often. Add chicken and heat through.                                   *Serves 4*

**tip**

For 2 cups cubed cooked chicken: In medium saucepan over medium heat, in 4 cups boiling water, cook 1 pound skinless, boneless chicken breasts *or* thighs, cubed, 5 minutes or until chicken is no longer pink. Chicken should be cooked to a minimum internal temperature of 165°F.

*25-Minute Chicken & Noodles*

# Chicken Mozzarella

**Prep Time:** 10 minutes    **Cook Time:** 20 minutes

4 skinless, boneless chicken breast halves (about 1 pound)
1 can (10¾ ounces) CAMPBELL'S HEALTHY REQUEST Condensed Tomato Soup
½ teaspoon Italian seasoning *or* dried oregano leaves, crushed
½ teaspoon garlic powder
¼ cup shredded mozzarella cheese (1 ounce)
4 cups hot cooked corkscrew macaroni (about 3 cups uncooked), cooked without salt

**1.** Place chicken in 2-quart shallow baking dish. Mix soup, Italian seasoning and garlic powder. Spoon over chicken and bake at 400°F. for 20 minutes or until chicken is no longer pink.

**2.** Sprinkle cheese over chicken. Remove chicken. Stir sauce. Serve with macaroni.                    *Serves 4*

**Nutritional Values per Serving:** Calories 559, Total Fat 7g, Saturated Fat 2g, Cholesterol 78mg, Sodium 385mg, Total Carbohydrate 80g, Protein 41g

## QUICK SIDE DISH Simple Seasoned Pasta

**Prep Time:** 5 minutes    **Cook Time:** 15 minutes

1 can (14½ ounces) SWANSON Seasoned Chicken Broth with Italian Herbs
1½ cups *uncooked* corkscrew macaroni

In medium saucepan over medium-high heat, heat broth to a boil. Stir in macaroni. **Reduce heat to medium.** Simmer gently 10 minutes or until macaroni is done, stirring occasionally.    *Serves 2*

*Chicken Mozzarella and Simple Seasoned Pasta*

# Texas Two-Step Chicken Picante

**Prep Time:** 5 minutes     **Cook Time:** 20 minutes

4 skinless, boneless chicken breast halves
1½ cups PACE Picante Sauce *or* Thick & Chunky Salsa
3 tablespoons packed light brown sugar
1 tablespoon Dijon-style mustard

**1.** Place chicken in 2-quart shallow baking dish. Mix picante sauce, sugar and mustard. Pour over chicken.

**2.** Bake at 400°F. for 20 minutes or until chicken is no longer pink. Serve with hot cooked rice if desired. *Serves 4*

# Honey-Mustard Chicken

*(photo on page 15)*
**Prep Time:** 10 minutes     **Cook Time:** 20 minutes

1 tablespoon butter *or* margarine
4 skinless, boneless chicken breast halves
1 can (10¾ ounces) CAMPBELL'S Condensed Cream of Chicken Soup *or* 98% Fat Free Cream of Chicken Soup
¼ cup mayonnaise
2 tablespoons honey
1 tablespoon spicy brown mustard
Chopped toasted pecans *or* walnuts

**1.** In medium skillet over medium-high heat, heat butter. Add chicken and cook 10 minutes or until browned. Set chicken aside.

**2.** Add soup, mayonnaise, honey and mustard. Heat to a boil. Return chicken to pan. Reduce heat to low. Cover and cook 5 minutes or until chicken is no longer pink. Sprinkle with pecans. Serve with rice if desired. *Serves 4*

*Top to bottom: Mexican-Style Mac 'n' Cheese (page 51), Queso Baked Potato (page 76) and Texas Two-Step Chicken Picante*

# Chicken Dijon

**Prep Time:** 5 minutes     **Cook Time:** 20 minutes

Vegetable cooking spray

4 skinless, boneless chicken breast halves (about 1 pound)

1 can (10¾ ounces) CAMPBELL'S Condensed Cream of Celery Soup *or* 98% Fat Free Cream of Celery Soup

⅔ cup water

1 tablespoon Dijon-style mustard

⅛ teaspoon pepper

4 cups hot cooked rice

1. Spray medium skillet with cooking spray and heat over medium-high heat 1 minute. Add chicken and cook 10 minutes or until browned. Set chicken aside.

2. Add soup, water, mustard and pepper. Heat to a boil. Return chicken to pan. Reduce heat to low. Cover and cook 5 minutes or until chicken is no longer pink. Serve with rice.     *Serves 4*

## tip

The versatile Vegetable Stir-Fry (page 51), pictured right as a side dish, also works as a main dish served over rice.

*Left to right: Vegetable Stir-Fry (page 51) and Chicken Dijon*

# Santa Fe Chicken

**Prep Time:** 10 minutes    **Cook Time:** 20 minutes

>  1 tablespoon all-purpose flour
>  1 tablespoon chili powder
>  4 skinless, boneless chicken breast halves (about 1 pound)
>  2 tablespoons vegetable oil
>  1 can (10¾ ounces) CAMPBELL'S Condensed Tomato Soup
>  ¼ cup shredded Cheddar *or* Monterey Jack cheese (1 ounce)

**1.** Mix flour and chili powder. Coat chicken with flour mixture.

**2.** In medium skillet over medium heat, heat oil. Add chicken and cook 10 minutes or until browned. Set chicken aside. Pour off fat.

**3.** Add soup. Heat to a boil. Return chicken to pan. Reduce heat to low. Cover and cook 5 minutes or until chicken is no longer pink. Sprinkle with cheese.

*Serves 4*

## QUICK SIDE DISH Simple Two-Step Nacho Pasta

**Prep Time:** 5 minutes    **Cook Time:** 20 minutes

>  4 cups *uncooked* corkscrew macaroni
>  1 can (11 ounces) CAMPBELL'S Condensed Fiesta Nacho Cheese Soup
>  ½ cup milk

**1.** In large saucepan prepare macaroni according to package directions. Drain.

**2.** In same pan mix soup, milk and macaroni. Over medium heat, heat through, stirring often.

*Serves 4*

Left to right: *Simple Two-Step Nacho Pasta and Santa Fe Chicken*

# Crispy Chicken with Asparagus Sauce

**Prep Time:** 10 minutes     **Cook Time:** 20 minutes

4 skinless, boneless chicken breast halves *or*
   8 skinless, boneless chicken thighs (about
   1 pound)
1 egg *or* 2 egg whites, beaten
½ cup dry bread crumbs
2 tablespoons vegetable oil
1 can (10¾ ounces) CAMPBELL'S Condensed Cream
   of Asparagus Soup
⅓ cup milk
⅓ cup water
   Grated Parmesan cheese

**1.** Dip chicken into egg. Coat with bread crumbs.

**2.** In medium skillet over medium heat, heat oil. Add chicken and cook 15 minutes or until chicken is browned and no longer pink. Remove and keep warm. Pour off fat.

**3.** Add soup, milk and water. Reduce heat to low and heat through. Serve over chicken. Sprinkle with cheese. Serve with rice if desired.                                      *Serves 4*

Top to bottom: *Crispy Chicken with Asparagus Sauce
and Quick Lemon-Broccoli Rice (page 79)*

# MEAT DISHES IN MINUTES

## Shortcut Beef Stew

**Prep Time:** 5 minutes     **Cook Time:** 25 minutes

- 1 **tablespoon vegetable oil**
- 1 **pound boneless beef sirloin steak, cut into 1-inch cubes**
- 1 **can (10¾ ounces) CAMPBELL'S Condensed Tomato Soup**
- 1 **can (10¾ ounces) CAMPBELL'S Condensed Beefy Mushroom Soup**
- 1 **tablespoon Worcestershire sauce**
- 1 **bag (24 ounces) frozen vegetables for stew (potatoes, carrots, celery)**

**1.** In Dutch oven over medium-high heat, heat oil. Add beef and cook until browned, stirring often. Set beef aside.

**2.** Add soups, Worcestershire and vegetables. Heat to a boil. Return beef to pan. Reduce heat to low. Cover and cook 10 minutes or until vegetables are tender, stirring occasionally.

*Serves 4*

*Shortcut Beef Stew*

# Easy Spaghetti & Meatballs

**Prep Time:** 15 minutes     **Cook Time:** 10 minutes

> 1 pound ground beef
> 2 tablespoons water
> ⅓ cup seasoned dry bread crumbs
> 1 egg, beaten
> 1 jar (28 ounces) PREGO Traditional Pasta Sauce *or* Pasta Sauce Flavored with Meat
> 4 cups hot cooked spaghetti

**1.** Mix beef, water, bread crumbs and egg. Shape meat mixture into 12 (2-inch) meatballs. Arrange in 2-quart shallow microwave-safe baking dish.

**2.** Microwave on HIGH 5 minutes or until meatballs are no longer pink (160°F.). Pour off fat. Pour pasta sauce over meatballs. Cover and microwave 3 minutes more or until sauce is hot. Serve over spaghetti.                    *Serves 4*

# Zesty Ziti

**Prep Time:** 10 minutes     **Cook Time:** 20 minutes

> 1 pound Italian sausage, cut into ½-inch pieces
> 1 large onion, chopped (about 1 cup)
> 1 medium green pepper, diced (about 1 cup)
> 1 jar (28 ounces) PREGO Three Cheese Pasta Sauce
> 4½ cups hot cooked medium tube-shaped macaroni

**1.** In medium skillet over medium heat, cook sausage, onion and pepper until sausage is no longer pink. Pour off fat.

**2.** Add pasta sauce. Heat to a boil. Serve over macaroni. Top with grated Parmesan cheese.                    *Serves 4*

Top to bottom: *Zesty Ziti and Easy Spaghetti & Meatballs*

# Fiesta Taco Salad

**Prep Time:** 10 minutes    **Cook Time:** 15 minutes

1 **pound ground beef**
2 **tablespoons chili powder**
1 **can (10¾ ounces) CAMPBELL'S Condensed Tomato
  Soup**
8 **cups salad greens torn into bite-size pieces**
2 **cups tortilla chips**
  **Chopped tomato**
  **Sliced green onions**
  **Shredded Cheddar cheese**
  **Sliced pitted ripe olives**

**1.** In medium skillet over medium-high heat, cook beef and chili
powder until beef is browned, stirring to separate meat. Pour
off fat.

**2.** Add soup. Reduce heat to low and heat through.

**3.** Arrange salad greens and chips on platter. Spoon meat mixture
over salad greens. Top with tomato, onions, cheese and olives.

*Serves 4*

**timesaver tip**

Save time by using packaged pre-shredded
Cheddar cheese and checking the salad bar at
your supermarket for pre-cut greens, toppers
and trimmings.

*Fiesta Taco Salad*

# Two-Bean Chili

**Prep Time:** 10 minutes  **Cook Time:** 15 minutes

1 **pound ground beef**
1 **large green pepper, chopped (about 1 cup)**
1 **large onion, chopped (about 1 cup)**
2 **tablespoons chili powder**
¼ **teaspoon black pepper**
3 **cups CAMPBELL'S Tomato Juice**
1 **can (about 15 ounces) kidney beans, rinsed and drained**
1 **can (about 15 ounces) great Northern** *or* **white kidney (cannellini) beans, rinsed and drained**
  **Sour cream**
  **Sliced green onions**
  **Shredded Cheddar cheese**
  **Chopped tomato**

1. In medium skillet over medium-high heat, cook beef, green pepper, onion, chili powder and black pepper until beef is browned, stirring to separate meat. Pour off fat.

2. Add tomato juice and beans and heat through. Top with sour cream, green onions, cheese and tomato.          *Serves 6*

**tip**

For a cool refresher, mix ¾ cup CAMPBELL'S Tomato Juice with ¼ cup ginger ale and 1 tablespoon lemon juice. Serve over ice and garnish with lemon slice.

*Top to bottom: Hearty Vegetarian Chili (page 50) and Two-Bean Chili*

# Spicy Salsa Mac & Beef

**Prep Time:** 5 minutes    **Cook Time:** 25 minutes

> 1 **pound ground beef**
> 1 **can (10½ ounces) CAMPBELL'S Condensed Beef Broth**
> 1⅓ **cups water**
> 2 **cups** *uncooked* **medium shell** *or* **elbow macaroni**
> 1 **can (10¾ ounces) CAMPBELL'S Condensed Cheddar Cheese Soup**
> 1 **cup PACE Thick & Chunky Salsa**

**1.** In medium skillet over medium-high heat, cook beef until browned, stirring to separate meat. Pour off fat.

**2.** Add broth and water. Heat to a boil. Stir in macaroni. Reduce heat to medium. Cook 10 minutes or until macaroni is done, stirring often.

**3.** Stir in soup and salsa and heat through.        *Serves 4*

## tip

Pair this dynamic kid-pleasing dish with a glass of V8 SPLASH. The light taste of tropical fruit juices makes a great go-with and delivers 100% of Vitamins A and C.

*Spicy Salsa Mac & Beef*

# Quick Pepper Steak

**Prep Time:** 10 minutes     **Cook Time:** 20 minutes

> 1 pound boneless beef sirloin *or* top round steak,
> ¾ inch thick
> 2 tablespoons vegetable oil
> 2 medium green *or* red peppers, cut into 2-inch-long
> strips (about 3 cups)
> 1 medium onion, cut into wedges
> ½ teaspoon garlic powder
> 1 can (10¼ ounces) FRANCO-AMERICAN Beef Gravy
> 1 tablespoon Worcestershire sauce
> 4 cups hot cooked rice

**1.** Slice beef into thin strips.

**2.** In medium skillet over medium-high heat, heat **half** the oil. Add beef in 2 batches and stir-fry until browned. Set beef aside.

**3.** Reduce heat to medium. Add remaining oil. Add peppers, onion and garlic powder and stir-fry until tender-crisp. Pour off fat.

**4.** Add gravy and Worcestershire. Heat to a boil. Return beef to pan. Reduce heat to low and heat through. Serve over rice.

*Serves 4*

## tip

Instead of choosing either green or red peppers,
try both together to vary the flavor and create
a colorful dish!

*Quick Pepper Steak*

# Southwest Skillet

**Prep/Cook Time:** 20 minutes     **Stand Time:** 5 minutes

¾ **pound ground beef**
1 **tablespoon chili powder**
1 **can (10¾ ounces) CAMPBELL'S Condensed Beefy Mushroom Soup**
¼ **cup water**
1 **can (about 15 ounces) kidney beans, rinsed and drained**
1 **can (14½ ounces) whole peeled tomatoes, cut up**
¾ **cup uncooked Minute® Original Rice**
½ **cup shredded Cheddar cheese (2 ounces)**
   **Crumbled tortilla chips**

**1.** In medium skillet over medium-high heat, cook beef and chili powder until browned, stirring to separate meat. Pour off fat.

**2.** Add soup, water, beans and tomatoes. Heat to a boil. Reduce heat to low. Cover and cook 10 minutes.

**3.** Stir in rice. Remove from heat. Cover and let stand 5 minutes. Top with cheese and chips.                    *Serves 4*

**tip**

Store ground meat in the coldest part of the refrigerator (40°F.) for up to 2 days. Be sure to cook ground meat thoroughly until browned, to a minimum 160°F.

Top to bottom: *Ham & Pasta Skillet (page 46) and Southwest Skillet*

# Mushroom Garlic Pork Chops

**Prep Time:** 5 minutes    **Cook Time:** 20 minutes

1 tablespoon vegetable oil
4 pork chops, ½ inch thick (about 1 pound)
1 can (10¾ ounces) CAMPBELL'S Condensed Cream
   of Mushroom with Roasted Garlic Soup
¼ cup water

**1.** In medium skillet over medium-high heat, heat oil. Add chops and cook 10 minutes or until browned. Set chops aside. Pour off fat.

**2.** Add soup and water. Heat to a boil. Return chops to pan. Reduce heat to low. Cover and cook 5 minutes or until chops are no longer pink.                    *Serves 4*

# Ham & Pasta Skillet

*(photo on page 45)*
**Prep Time:** 10 minutes    **Cook Time:** 15 minutes

1 can (10¾ ounces) CAMPBELL'S Condensed Broccoli
   Cheese Soup
1 cup milk
1 tablespoon spicy brown mustard
2 cups broccoli flowerets *or* 1 package (10 ounces)
   frozen broccoli cuts (2 cups)
1½ cups cooked ham strips
3 cups cooked medium shell macaroni (about 2 cups
   uncooked)

In medium skillet mix soup, milk, mustard and broccoli. Over medium heat, heat to a boil. Reduce heat to low. Cook 5 minutes or until broccoli is tender. Add ham and macaroni and heat through.

*Serves 4*

*Mushroom Garlic Pork Chop*

# Campbell's
# EASY FISH & MEATLESS

## Garlic Shrimp & Pasta

**Prep Time:** 15 minutes     **Cook Time:** 10 minutes

> 1 can (14½ ounces) SWANSON Chicken Broth (1¾ cups)
> 2 cloves garlic, minced
> 3 tablespoons chopped fresh parsley *or* 1 tablespoon dried parsley flakes
> 2 tablespoons cornstarch
> 2 tablespoons lemon juice
> ⅛ teaspoon ground red pepper
> 1 pound medium shrimp, shelled and deveined
> 4 cups hot cooked thin spaghetti (about 8 ounces uncooked)

1. In medium saucepan mix broth, garlic, parsley, cornstarch, lemon juice and pepper. Over medium-high heat, heat to a boil. Cook until mixture thickens, stirring constantly.

2. Add shrimp. Cook 5 minutes more or until shrimp turn pink, stirring often. Toss with spaghetti.                    *Serves 4*

Top to bottom: *Quick 'n' Easy Salmon (page 50), Vegetable-Rice Pilaf (page 78) and Garlic Shrimp & Pasta*

# Quick 'n' Easy Salmon

*(photo on page 49)*
**Prep Time:** 5 minutes    **Cook Time:** 15 minutes

    1 can (14½ ounces) SWANSON Chicken Broth
      (1¾ cups)
 ¼ cup Chablis *or* other dry white wine
 ¼ teaspoon dried dill weed, crushed
    4 thin lemon slices
    4 salmon steaks, 1 inch thick (about 1½ pounds)

**1.** In medium skillet mix broth, wine, dill and lemon. Over medium-high heat, heat to a boil.

**2.** Place fish in broth mixture. Reduce heat to low. Cover and cook 10 minutes or until fish flakes easily when tested with a fork. Discard poaching liquid.     *Serves 4*

# Hearty Vegetarian Chili

*(photo on page 39)*
**Prep Time:** 10 minutes    **Cook Time:** 20 minutes

    2 tablespoons vegetable oil
    1 large onion, chopped (about 1 cup)
    1 small green pepper, chopped (about ½ cup)
 ¼ teaspoon garlic powder *or* 2 cloves garlic, minced
    1 tablespoon chili powder
 ½ teaspoon ground cumin
2½ cups V8 100% Vegetable Juice
    1 can (16 ounces) black beans, rinsed and drained
    1 can (15 ounces) pinto beans, rinsed and drained

**1.** In large saucepan over medium heat, heat oil. Add onion, pepper, garlic powder, chili powder and cumin and cook until tender.

**2.** Add vegetable juice. Heat to a boil. Reduce heat to low. Cook 5 minutes. Add beans and heat through.     *Serves 4*

# Vegetable Stir-Fry

*(photo on page 27)*
**Prep Time:** 15 minutes    **Cook Time:** 10 minutes

> 1 can (14½ ounces) SWANSON Vegetable Broth
> 2 tablespoons cornstarch
> 1 tablespoon soy sauce
> ¼ teaspoon ground ginger
> 1 tablespoon vegetable oil
> 5 cups cut-up vegetables*
> ⅛ teaspoon garlic powder *or* 1 clove garlic, minced

**1.** In bowl mix broth, cornstarch, soy sauce and ginger until smooth. Set aside.

**2.** In medium skillet over medium-high heat, heat oil. Add vegetables and garlic powder and stir-fry until tender-crisp.

**3.** Stir cornstarch mixture and add. Cook until mixture boils and thickens, stirring constantly.

*Serves 4 as a main dish or 8 as a side dish*

*\*Use a combination of broccoli flowerets, sliced mushrooms, sliced carrots, sliced celery, red or green pepper strips and sliced green onions.*

# Mexican-Style Mac 'n' Cheese

*(photo on page 25)*
**Prep Time:** 5 minutes    **Cook Time:** 10 minutes

> 2 cups *uncooked* elbow macaroni
> 1 jar (15 ounces) PACE Picante con Queso Dip

**1.** In large saucepan prepare macaroni according to package directions. Drain.

**2.** In same pan mix dip and macaroni. Over low heat, heat through, stirring occasionally.

*Serves 4*

# Cajun Fish

**Prep Time:** 10 minutes     **Cook Time:** 15 minutes

> 1 tablespoon vegetable oil
> 1 small green pepper, diced (about ⅔ cup)
> ½ teaspoon dried oregano leaves, crushed
> 1 can (10¾ ounces) CAMPBELL'S Condensed Tomato Soup
> ⅓ cup water
> ⅛ teaspoon garlic powder
> ⅛ teaspoon black pepper
> ⅛ teaspoon ground red pepper
> 1 pound firm white fish fillets (cod, haddock or halibut)

**1.** In medium skillet over medium heat, heat oil. Add green pepper and oregano and cook until tender-crisp, stirring often. Add soup, water, garlic powder, black pepper and red pepper. Heat to a boil.

**2.** Place fish in soup mixture. Reduce heat to low. Cover and cook 5 minutes or until fish flakes easily when tested with a fork. Serve with rice if desired.                    *Serves 4*

*Cajun Fish*

# Primavera Fish Fillets

**Prep Time:** 10 minutes    **Cook Time:** 20 minutes

1 large carrot, cut into matchstick-thin strips (about 1 cup)
2 stalks celery, cut into matchstick-thin strips (about 1 cup)
1 small onion, diced (about ¼ cup)
¼ cup water
2 tablespoons Chablis *or* other dry white wine
½ teaspoon dried thyme leaves, crushed
    Generous dash pepper
1 can (10¾ ounces) **CAMPBELL'S HEALTHY REQUEST** Condensed Cream of Mushroom Soup
1 pound firm white fish fillets (cod, haddock or halibut)

**1.** In medium skillet mix carrot, celery, onion, water, wine, thyme and pepper. Over medium-high heat, heat to a boil. Reduce heat to low. Cover and cook 5 minutes or until vegetables are tender-crisp.

**2.** Stir in soup. Over medium heat, heat to a boil.

**3.** Place fish in soup mixture. Reduce heat to low. Cover and cook 5 minutes or until fish flakes easily when tested with a fork.

*Serves 4*

**Nutritional Values per Serving:** Calories 152, Total Fat 2g, Saturated Fat 1g, Cholesterol 45mg, Sodium 414mg, Total Carbohydrate 11g, Protein 1

In this recipe, CAMPBELL'S HEALTHY REQUEST creates a lower fat alternative to a traditional Newburg-style sauce made with butter and cream.

*Primavera Fish Fillet*

# Seafood & Mushroom Shells

**Bake Time:** 30 minutes*    **Prep/Cook Time:** 20 minutes

> 1 package (10 ounces) PEPPERIDGE FARM Frozen
>   Puff Pastry Shells
> 4 tablespoons unsalted butter
> 2½ cups thinly sliced mushrooms (about 8 ounces)
> 1 can (10¾ ounces) CAMPBELL'S Condensed Cream
>   of Mushroom Soup *or* 98% Fat Free Cream of
>   Mushroom Soup
> ½ cup dry white wine *or* vermouth
> 1 tablespoon lemon juice
> 1 pound firm white fish (cod, haddock or halibut),
>   cut into 1-inch pieces
> ½ cup grated Parmesan cheese

**1.** Bake pastry shells according to package directions.

**2.** In medium skillet over medium heat, heat butter. Add mushrooms and cook until tender.

**3.** Add soup, wine, lemon juice and fish. Cook 5 minutes or until fish flakes easily when tested with a fork.

**4.** Serve in pastry shells. Sprinkle with cheese.              *Serves 4*

*Bake pastry shells while preparing fish mixture.*

Top to bottom: *Seafood & Mushroom Shells
and Creamy Vegetables in Pastry Shells (page 76)*

# SPEEDY SNACKS & MINI-MEALS

## Chicken Noodle Soup Express

**Prep Time:** 10 minutes      **Cook Time:** 15 minutes

2 cans (14½ ounces *each*) SWANSON Chicken Broth (3½ cups)
    Generous dash pepper
1 medium carrot, sliced (about ½ cup)
1 stalk celery, sliced (about ½ cup)
½ cup *uncooked* medium egg noodles
1 can (5 ounces) SWANSON Premium Chunk Chicken Breast *or* Chunk Chicken, drained

In medium saucepan mix broth, pepper, carrot and celery. Over medium-high heat, heat to a boil. Stir in noodles. Reduce heat to medium. Cook 10 minutes, stirring often. Add chicken and heat through.                                    *Serves 4*

*Top to bottom: Easy Vegetable Soup (page 60) and Chicken Noodle Soup Express*

58

# Easy Vegetable Soup

*(photo on page 59)*
**Prep Time:** 5 minutes    **Cook Time:** 25 minutes

> 2 cans (14½ ounces *each*) SWANSON Chicken Broth (3½ cups)
> 3 cups CAMPBELL'S Tomato Juice
> 1 teaspoon dried oregano leaves *or* Italian seasoning, crushed
> ½ teaspoon garlic powder *or* 4 cloves garlic, minced
> ¼ teaspoon pepper
> 1 bag (16 ounces) frozen vegetable combination (broccoli, cauliflower, carrots)
> 1 can (about 15 ounces) kidney beans *or* 1 can (about 16 ounces) white kidney (cannellini) beans, rinsed and drained

In large saucepan mix broth, tomato juice, oregano, garlic powder, pepper and vegetables. Over medium-high heat, heat to a boil. Cover and cook 10 minutes or until vegetables are tender. Add beans and heat through.                    *Serves 8*

**tip**

For a change of taste, substitute 1 bag (16 ounces) frozen Italian vegetable combination.

# Mushroom Mozzarella Bruschetta

*(photo on page 9)*

**Prep Time:** 15 minutes     **Cook Time:** 5 minutes

1 loaf (about 1 pound) Italian bread (16 inches long),
  cut in half lengthwise
1 can (10¾ ounces) CAMPBELL'S Condensed Cream
  of Mushroom Soup *or* 98% Fat Free Cream of
  Mushroom Soup
¼ teaspoon garlic powder
¼ teaspoon dried Italian seasoning, crushed
1 cup shredded mozzarella cheese (4 ounces)
1 tablespoon grated Parmesan cheese
1 small red pepper, chopped (about ½ cup)
2 green onions, chopped (about ¼ cup)

**1.** Bake bread on baking sheet at 400°F. for 5 minutes or until lightly toasted.

**2.** Mix soup, garlic powder and Italian seasoning. Stir in mozzarella cheese, Parmesan cheese, pepper and onions.

**3.** Spread soup mixture on bread. Bake 5 minutes or until cheese is melted. Cut each bread half into 4 pieces.          *Serves 8*

## timesaver tip

For convenience, use packaged pre-shredded mozzarella cheese. Half an 8-ounce package will provide the 1 cup needed for this recipe.

# Chicken Broccoli Pockets

**Prep Time:** 15 minutes     **Cook Time:** 10 minutes

1 can (10¾ ounces) CAMPBELL'S HEALTHY REQUEST
   Condensed Cream of Chicken Soup
¼ cup water
1 tablespoon lemon juice
¼ teaspoon garlic powder
⅛ teaspoon pepper
1 cup cooked broccoli flowerets
1 medium carrot, shredded (about ½ cup)
2 cups cubed cooked chicken
3 pita breads (6-inch), cut in half, forming 2 pockets

**1.** In medium saucepan mix soup, water, lemon juice, garlic powder, pepper, broccoli, carrot and chicken. Over medium heat, heat through.

**2.** Spoon ½ cup chicken mixture into each pita half.

*Makes 6 sandwiches*

**Nutritional Values per Serving:** Calories 202, Total Fat 4g, Saturated Fat 1g, Cholesterol 39mg, Sodium 404mg, Total Carbohydrate 24g, Protein 16g

**Chicken Broccoli Potato Topper:** Omit pita breads. Serve ¾ cup chicken mixture over each of 4 hot baked potatoes, split (about 2 pounds). *Serves 4*

In this recipe, CAMPBELL'S HEALTHY REQUEST provides a healthier, delicious alternative to a mayonnaise-based pocket sandwich filling.

*Top to bottom: Creamy Risotto (page 80) and Chicken Broccoli Pocket*

# Souperburger Sandwiches

**Prep Time:** 5 minutes  **Cook Time:** 10 minutes

> 1 **pound ground beef**
> 1 **medium onion, chopped (about ½ cup)**
> 1 **can (10¾ ounces) CAMPBELL'S Condensed Cheddar Cheese Soup**
> 1 **tablespoon prepared mustard**
> ⅛ **teaspoon pepper**
> 6 **hamburger rolls, split and toasted**

**1.** In medium skillet over medium-high heat, cook beef and onion until beef is browned, stirring to separate meat. Pour off fat.

**2.** Add soup, mustard and pepper. Reduce heat to low and heat through. Divide meat mixture among rolls.

*Makes 6 sandwiches*

# Sausage & Pepper Sandwiches

**Prep Time:** 10 minutes  **Cook Time:** 10 minutes

> 1 **pound bulk pork sausage**
> 1 **small green pepper, chopped (about ½ cup)**
> 1 **can (11⅛ ounces) CAMPBELL'S Condensed Italian Tomato Soup**
> 4 **long sandwich rolls, split**

**1.** In medium skillet over medium-high heat, cook sausage and pepper until sausage is browned, stirring to separate meat. Pour off fat.

**2.** Add soup. Reduce heat to low and heat through. Divide meat mixture among rolls.

*Makes 4 sandwiches*

*Top to bottom: Souperburger Sandwich, Sausage & Pepper Sandwich and Shortcut Sloppy Joe (page 66)*

# 5-Minute Burrito Wraps

**Prep/Cook Time:** 5 minutes

1 can (11¼ ounces) CAMPBELL'S Condensed Fiesta
　　Chili Beef Soup
6 flour tortillas (8-inch)
　　Shredded Cheddar cheese

**1.** Spoon 2 tablespoons soup down center of each tortilla. Top with cheese. Fold tortilla around filling.

**2.** Place seam-side down on microwave-safe plate and microwave on HIGH 2 minutes or until hot.　　　*Makes 6 burritos*

# Shortcut Sloppy Joes

*(photo on page 65)*
**Prep Time:** 5 minutes　　**Cook Time:** 10 minutes

　1 pound ground beef
　1 can (11⅛ ounces) CAMPBELL'S Condensed Italian
　　　Tomato Soup
¼ cup water
　2 teaspoons Worcestershire sauce
⅛ teaspoon pepper
　6 hamburger rolls, split and toasted

**1.** In medium skillet over medium-high heat, cook beef until browned, stirring to separate meat. Pour off fat.

**2.** Add soup, water, Worcestershire and pepper. Reduce heat to low and heat through. Divide meat mixture among rolls.
　　　*Makes 6 sandwiches*

*5-Minute Burrito Wraps*

# Quick Beef 'n' Beans Tacos

**Prep Time:** 15 minutes     **Cook Time:** 10 minutes

> 1 pound ground beef
> 1 small onion, chopped (about ¼ cup)
> 1 can (11¼ ounces) CAMPBELL'S Condensed Fiesta
>    Chili Beef Soup
> ¼ cup water
> 10 taco shells
>    Shredded Cheddar cheese, shredded lettuce,
>    diced tomato and sour cream

**1.** In medium skillet over medium-high heat, cook beef and onion until beef is browned, stirring to separate meat. Pour off fat.

**2.** Add soup and water. Reduce heat to low. Cover and cook 5 minutes.

**3.** Divide meat mixture among taco shells. Top with cheese, lettuce, tomato and sour cream.     *Makes 10 tacos*

# Deluxe Nachos

**Prep Time:** 10 minutes     **Cook Time:** 5 minutes

> 1 can (about 16 ounces) black beans, drained
> 1 bag (about 9 ounces) tortilla chips
> 1 jar (15 ounces) PACE Picante con Queso Dip
> 1 medium tomato, chopped (about 1 cup)
> ¼ cup sliced pitted ripe olives
> 2 green onions, sliced (about ¼ cup)

Spread beans over tortilla chips. Heat dip according to package directions. Spoon over tortilla chips. Top with tomato, olives and onions.     *Serves 6*

*Top to bottom: Deluxe Nachos and Quick Beef 'n' Beans Tacos*

# Cheesy Broccoli Potato Topper

**Prep Time:** 5 minutes     **Cook Time:** 5 minutes

> 1 can (10¾ ounces) CAMPBELL'S Condensed
>     Cheddar Cheese Soup
> 4 large hot baked potatoes, split
> 1 cup cooked broccoli flowerets

**1.** Stir soup in can until soup is smooth.

**2.** Place hot baked potatoes on microwave-safe plate. Carefully fluff up potatoes with fork.

**3.** Top each potato with broccoli. Spoon soup over potatoes. Microwave on HIGH 4 minutes or until hot.      *Serves 4*

# Baked Potatoes Olé

**Prep Time:** 5 minutes     **Cook Time:** 15 minutes

> 1 pound ground beef
> 1 tablespoon chili powder
> 1 cup PACE Picante Sauce *or* Thick & Chunky Salsa
> 4 hot baked potatoes, split
>     Shredded Cheddar cheese

**1.** In medium skillet over medium-high heat, cook beef and chili powder until beef is browned, stirring to separate meat. Pour off fat.

**2.** Add picante sauce. Reduce heat to low and heat through. Serve over potatoes. Top with cheese.      *Serves 4*

Clockwise from top: *Cheesy Picante Potatoes (page 77),
Baked Potato Olé and Cheesy Broccoli Potato Topper*

# Campbell's
# QUICK SIDE DISHES

## One-Dish Pasta & Vegetables

**Prep Time:** 15 minutes     **Cook Time:** 15 minutes

1½ cups *uncooked* corkscrew macaroni
2 medium carrots, sliced (about 1 cup)
1 cup broccoli flowerets
1 can (10¾ ounces) CAMPBELL'S Condensed
    Cheddar Cheese Soup
½ cup milk
1 tablespoon prepared mustard

**1.** In large saucepan prepare macaroni according to package directions. Add carrots and broccoli for last 5 minutes of cooking time. Drain.

**2.** In same pan mix soup, milk, mustard and macaroni mixture. Over medium heat, heat through, stirring often.     *Serves 5*

*One-Dish Pasta & Vegetables*

# Quick Onion Fries

**Prep Time:** 5 minutes  **Cook Time:** about 20 minutes

> 1 pouch CAMPBELL'S Dry Onion Soup and Recipe Mix
> 3 tablespoons vegetable oil
> 1 package (about 22 ounces) frozen French-fried potatoes

**1.** In large bowl mix soup mix and oil. Add potatoes. Toss to coat.

**2.** Bake according to package directions, stirring occasionally.

*Serves 6*

# Saucy Asparagus

**Prep Time:** 10 minutes  **Cook Time:** 15 minutes

> 1 can (10¾ ounces) CAMPBELL'S Condensed Cream of Asparagus Soup
> 2 tablespoons milk
> 1½ pounds asparagus, trimmed, cut into 1-inch pieces (about 3 cups) *or* 2 packages (10 ounces *each*) frozen asparagus cuts

**1.** In medium saucepan mix soup and milk. Over medium heat, heat to a boil, stirring occasionally.

**2.** Add asparagus. Reduce heat to low. Cover and cook 10 minutes or until asparagus is tender, stirring occasionally.  *Serves 6*

Top to bottom: *Quick Onion Fries and Saucy Asparagus*

# Queso Baked Potatoes

*(photo on page 25)*
**Prep Time:** 10 minutes     **Cook Time:** 3 minutes

**4 hot baked potatoes, split**
**1 cup PACE Picante con Queso Dip**

**1.** Place hot baked potatoes on microwave-safe plate. Carefully fluff up potatoes with fork.

**2.** Spoon dip over potatoes. Microwave on HIGH 3 minutes or until hot.                                              *Serves 4*

**To heat one potato:** Top with ¼ cup dip. Microwave on HIGH 1 minute or until hot. Increase time to 2 minutes if using dip from the refrigerator.

# Creamy Vegetables in Pastry Shells

*(photo on page 57)*
**Bake Time:** 30 minutes     **Prep/Cook Time:** 15 minutes

**1 package (10 ounces) PEPPERIDGE FARM Frozen Puff Pastry Shells**
**1 can (10¾ ounces) CAMPBELL'S Condensed Cream of Mushroom Soup *or* 98% Fat Free Cream of Mushroom Soup**
**⅓ cup milk *or* water**
**1 bag (16 ounces) frozen vegetable combination (broccoli, cauliflower, carrots), cooked and drained**

**1.** Prepare pastry shells according to package directions.

**2.** In medium saucepan mix soup and milk. Over medium heat, heat through, stirring often. Divide vegetables among pastry shells. Spoon sauce over pastry shells.                     *Serves 6*

# Garlic Mashed Potatoes

*(photo on page 17)*
**Prep Time:** 10 minutes     **Cook Time:** 15 minutes

**2 cans (14½ ounces *each*) SWANSON Seasoned
Chicken Broth with Roasted Garlic
5 large potatoes, cut into 1-inch pieces**

1. In medium saucepan place broth and potatoes. Over high heat, heat to a boil. Reduce heat to medium. Cover and cook 10 minutes or until potatoes are tender. Drain, reserving broth.

2. Mash potatoes with *1¼ cups* reserved broth. If needed, add additional broth until potatoes are desired consistency.

*Serves about 6*

**Skinny Mashed Potatoes:** Substitute 2 cans (14½ ounces *each*) SWANSON Chicken Broth for Chicken Broth with Roasted Garlic.

# Cheesy Picante Potatoes

*(photo on page 71)*
**Prep Time:** 10 minutes     **Cook Time:** 10 minutes

**1 can (10¾ ounces) CAMPBELL'S Condensed
    Cheddar Cheese Soup
½ cup PACE Picante Sauce *or* Thick & Chunky Salsa
1 teaspoon garlic powder
4 cups cubed cooked potatoes (about 4 medium)
    Paprika
2 tablespoons chopped fresh cilantro**

In medium skillet mix soup, picante sauce and garlic powder. Add potatoes. Over medium heat, heat through, stirring often. Sprinkle with paprika and cilantro. Serve with additional picante sauce.

*Serves 6 to 8*

# Vegetable-Rice Pilaf

*(photo on page 49)*

**Prep Time:** 5 minutes    **Cook Time:** 20 minutes

Vegetable cooking spray
¼ cup chopped green *or* red pepper
2 cloves garlic, minced
½ teaspoon dried basil leaves, crushed
⅛ teaspoon black pepper
1 cup *uncooked* regular long-grain white rice
1 can (16 ounces) CAMPBELL'S HEALTHY REQUEST Ready to Serve Chicken Broth
¾ cup frozen mixed vegetables

**1.** Spray medium skillet with cooking spray and heat over medium heat 1 minute. Add green pepper, garlic, basil, black pepper and rice. Cook until rice is browned and green pepper is tender-crisp, stirring constantly.

**2.** Stir in broth. Heat to a boil. Reduce heat to low. Cover and cook 10 minutes.

**3.** Stir in vegetables. Cover and cook 10 minutes more or until rice is done and most of liquid is absorbed.          *Serves 4*

**Nutritional Values per Serving:** Calories 204, Total Fat 1g, Saturated Fat 0g, Cholesterol 0mg, Sodium 241mg, Total Carbohydrate 43g, Protein 6g

Try this delicious side dish as a healthier alternative to high-sodium packaged rice dishes.

# Fiesta Rice

*(photo on page 5)*
**Prep Time:** 5 minutes    **Cook/Stand Time:** 10 minutes

> 1 can (10½ ounces) CAMPBELL'S Condensed Chicken Broth
> ½ cup water
> ½ cup PACE Thick & Chunky Salsa
> 2 cups uncooked Minute® Original Rice

**1.** In medium saucepan mix broth, water and salsa. Over medium-high heat, heat to a boil.

**2.** Stir in rice. Cover and remove from heat. Let stand 5 minutes. Fluff with fork.

*Serves 4*

# Quick Lemon-Broccoli Rice

*(photo on page 31)*
**Prep Time:** 10 minutes    **Cook Time:** 15 minutes

> 1 can (10½ ounces) CAMPBELL'S Condensed Chicken Broth
> 1 cup small broccoli flowerets
> 1 small carrot, shredded (about ⅓ cup)
> 1¼ cups uncooked Minute® Original Rice
> 2 teaspoons lemon juice
> Generous dash pepper

**1.** In medium saucepan over high heat, heat broth to a boil. Add broccoli and carrot. Reduce heat to low. Cover and cook 5 minutes or until vegetables are tender.

**2.** Stir in rice, lemon juice and pepper. Cover and remove from heat. Let stand 5 minutes. Fluff with fork.

*Serves 4*

# Creamy Risotto

*(photo on page 63)*

**Prep Time:** 5 minutes     **Cook/Stand Time:** 15 minutes

1 can (10¾ ounces) CAMPBELL'S HEALTHY REQUEST
    Condensed Cream of Mushroom Soup
1½ cups CAMPBELL'S HEALTHY REQUEST Ready to
    Serve Chicken Broth
1½ cups uncooked Minute® Original Rice
1 tablespoon grated Parmesan cheese
Pepper

**1.** In medium saucepan mix soup and broth. Over medium-high heat, heat to a boil.

**2.** Stir in rice and cheese. Cover and remove from heat. Let stand 10 minutes. Fluff with fork. Serve with freshly ground pepper and additional cheese if desired. *Serves 4*

**Nutritional Values per Serving:** Calories 191, Total Fat 2g, Saturated Fat 1g, Cholesterol 7mg, Sodium 480mg, Total Carbohydrate 36g, Protein 5g

**Tomato-Basil Risotto:** In step 2, add 1 tablespoon chopped fresh basil *or* ¼ teaspoon dried basil leaves, crushed, and 1 small tomato, diced (about ½ cup) *or* ½ cup drained cut-up canned tomatoes with rice.

**tip**

Use HEALTHY REQUEST to lighten up your favorite dishes such as this international specialty—easily and deliciously.

# Campbell's

# EVERYDAY EASY MEALS

# EVERYDAY EASY MEALS

For more delicious recipes and easy meal ideas, visit the
*Campbell's* Web site at **www.campbellsoup.com**

# Campbell's®

# Homemade in 20 Minutes

## CHICKEN & BROCCOLI ALFREDO

**Prep/Cook Time:** 20 minutes    *20 minutes or less!*

½ package *uncooked* linguine (8 ounces)
1 cup fresh *or* frozen broccoli flowerets
2 tablespoons butter *or* margarine
1 pound skinless, boneless chicken breasts, cubed
1 can (10¾ ounces) CAMPBELL'S Condensed Cream of Mushroom Soup *or* 98% Fat Free Cream of Mushroom Soup
½ cup milk
½ cup grated Parmesan cheese
¼ teaspoon freshly ground pepper

**1** Prepare linguine according to package directions. Add broccoli for last 4 minutes of cooking time.

**2** In medium skillet over medium-high heat, heat butter. Add chicken and cook until browned, stirring often. Drain.

**3** Add soup, milk, cheese, pepper and linguine mixture and cook through, stirring occasionally. Serve with additional Parmesan cheese.                        *Serves 4*

**Chicken & Broccoli Alfredo**

# 15-MINUTE CHICKEN & RICE DINNER

**Prep/Cook Time:** 15 minutes  *20 minutes or less!*

> 1 tablespoon vegetable oil
> 4 skinless, boneless chicken breast halves (about 1 pound)
> 1 can (10¾ ounces) CAMPBELL'S Condensed Cream of Chicken Soup *or* 98% Fat Free Cream of Chicken Soup
> 1½ cups water*
> ¼ teaspoon paprika
> ¼ teaspoon pepper
> 2 cups fresh *or* thawed frozen broccoli flowerets
> 1½ cups *uncooked* Minute® Original Rice

**1** In medium skillet over medium-high heat, heat oil. Add chicken and cook 8 minutes or until browned. Set chicken aside. Pour off fat.

**2** Add soup, water, paprika and pepper. Heat to a boil.

**3** Stir in broccoli and rice. Place chicken on rice mixture. Season chicken with additional paprika and pepper. Reduce heat to low. Cover and cook 5 minutes or until chicken is no longer pink.                                      *Serves 4*

**\*For creamier rice, increase water to 1⅔ cups.**

**15-Minute Chicken & Rice Dinner**

# 15-MINUTE HERBED CHICKEN

**Prep/Cook Time:** 15 minutes      *20 minutes or less!*

    1 tablespoon vegetable oil
    4 skinless, boneless chicken breast halves (about
        1 pound)
    1 can (10¾ ounces) CAMPBELL'S Condensed Cream of
        Chicken with Herbs Soup
    ½ cup milk
      Broth Simmered Rice*

**1** In medium skillet over medium-high heat, heat oil. Add chicken and cook 8 minutes or until browned. Set chicken aside. Pour off fat.

**2** Add soup and milk. Heat to a boil. Return chicken to pan. Reduce heat to low. Cover and cook 5 minutes or until chicken is no longer pink.

*Serves 4*

**\*Broth Simmered Rice:** In medium saucepan over medium-high heat, heat 1 can CAMPBELL'S Condensed Chicken Broth and 1 cup water to a boil. Stir in 2 cups *uncooked* Minute® Original Rice. Cover and remove from heat. Let stand 5 minutes. Fluff with fork.

**Creamy Mushroom-Garlic Chicken:** Substitute 1 can (10¾ ounces) CAMPBELL'S Condensed Cream of Mushroom with Roasted Garlic Soup for Cream of Chicken with Herbs Soup.

**Quick Herbed Chicken Dijon:** In step 2 add 1 tablespoon Dijon-style mustard with the soup and milk.

**Top to bottom: Hearty Chicken Noodle Soup (page 91), Broth Simmered Rice and 15-Minute Herbed Chicken**

# SPEEDY CHICKEN ENCHILADAS

**Prep/Cook Time:** 20 minutes   *20 minutes or less!*

1 pound skinless, boneless chicken breasts, cubed
1 can (10¾ ounces) CAMPBELL'S Condensed Cream of Chicken Soup *or* 98% Fat Free Cream of Chicken Soup
1 cup PACE Thick & Chunky Salsa *or* Picante Sauce
8 flour tortillas (6-inch)
1 can (10¾ ounces) CAMPBELL'S Condensed Cheddar Cheese Soup

**1** In medium nonstick skillet over medium-high heat, cook chicken until browned and juices evaporate, stirring often. Add chicken soup and ½ *cup* salsa. Heat to a boil, stirring occasionally.

**2** Along one side of each tortilla, spread about ⅓ *cup* chicken mixture. Roll up each tortilla around filling and place seam-side down in 2-quart microwave-safe baking dish.

**3** Mix cheese soup and remaining salsa and pour over enchiladas.

**4** Cover and microwave on HIGH 5 minutes or until hot.

*Serves 4*

*Warm tortillas for easier handling. Stack tortillas and wrap in damp, microwave-safe paper towels. Microwave on HIGH for 15 seconds for 2 tortillas; add 15 seconds to time for every 2 additional tortillas.*

**Top to bottom: Speedy Chicken Enchiladas and Beef & Cheddar Soft Tacos (page 90)**

## BEEF & CHEDDAR SOFT TACOS

*(photo on page 89)*

**Prep/Cook Time:** 15 minutes        *20 minutes or less!*

> 1 pound ground beef
> 1 can (10¾ ounces) CAMPBELL'S Condensed Cheddar
>     Cheese Soup
> ½ cup PACE Thick & Chunky Salsa *or* Picante Sauce
> 8 flour tortillas (8-inch)
> 2 cups shredded lettuce (about ½ small head)

**1** In medium skillet over medium-high heat, cook beef until browned, stirring to separate meat. Pour off fat.

**2** Add soup and salsa. Reduce heat to low and heat through.

**3** Spoon **about ⅓ cup** meat mixture down center of each tortilla. Top with lettuce. Fold tortilla around filling. Serve with additional salsa.

*Serves 4*

## SAUCY PORK CHOPS

*(photo on page 93)*

**Prep/Cook Time:** 15 minutes        *20 minutes or less!*

> 1 tablespoon vegetable oil
> 4 pork chops, ½ inch thick (about 1 pound)
> 1 can (10¾ ounces) CAMPBELL'S Condensed Cream of
>     Onion Soup
> ¼ cup water

**1** In medium skillet over medium-high heat, heat oil. Add chops and cook 8 minutes or until browned. Set chops aside. Pour off fat.

**2** Add soup and water. Heat to a boil. Return chops to pan. Reduce heat to low. Cover and cook 5 minutes or until chops are no longer pink.

*Serves 4*

# HEARTY CHICKEN NOODLE SOUP

*(photo on page 87)*

**Prep/Cook Time:** 20 minutes  *20 minutes or less!*

2 cans (10½ ounces *each*) CAMPBELL'S Condensed
    Chicken Broth
1 cup water
    Generous dash pepper
2 skinless, boneless chicken breast halves, cut up
1 medium carrot, sliced (about ½ cup)
1 stalk celery, sliced (about ½ cup)
½ cup *uncooked* medium egg noodles

**1** In medium saucepan mix broth, water, pepper, chicken, carrot and celery. Over medium-high heat, heat to a boil.

**2** Stir in noodles. Reduce heat to medium. Cook 10 minutes or until noodles are done, stirring often.

*Serves 4*

*Tip*   *Save time by using precut carrots and celery from your supermarket salad bar.*

# SEAFOOD TOMATO ALFREDO

*20 minutes or less!*

1 tablespoon margarine *or* butter
1 medium onion, chopped (about ½ cup)
1 can (10¾ ounces) CAMPBELL'S Condensed Cream of
    Mushroom with Roasted Garlic Soup
½ cup milk
1 cup diced canned tomatoes
1 pound firm white fish (cod, haddock *or* halibut), cut
    into 2-inch pieces
4 cups hot cooked linguine (about 8 ounces uncooked)

**1** In medium skillet over medium-high heat, heat margarine. Add onion and cook until tender.

**2** Add soup, milk and tomatoes. Heat to a boil. Add fish. Reduce heat to low. Cook 10 minutes or until fish flakes easily when tested with a fork. Serve over linguine.          *Serves 4*

---

*Tip* | *Salted water takes longer to boil. To save time, don't salt water until after it is boiling.*

**Top to bottom: Saucy Pork Chop (page 90) and
Seafood Tomato Alfredo**

## ASPARAGUS & HAM POTATO TOPPER

 **4 hot baked potatoes, split**
 **1 cup diced cooked ham**
 **1 can (10¾ ounces) CAMPBELL'S Condensed Cream of
    Asparagus Soup**
 **Shredded Cheddar *or* Swiss cheese (optional)**

**1** Place hot baked potatoes on microwave-safe plate. Carefully fluff up potatoes with fork.

**2** Top each potato with ham. Stir soup in can until smooth. Spoon soup over potatoes. Top with cheese, if desired. Microwave on HIGH 4 minutes or until hot.                               *Serves 4*

## LEMON ASPARAGUS CHICKEN

 **1 tablespoon vegetable oil**
 **4 skinless, boneless chicken breast halves (about
    1 pound)**
 **1 can (10¾ ounces) CAMPBELL'S Condensed Cream of
    Asparagus Soup**
 **¼ cup milk**
 **1 tablespoon lemon juice**
 **⅛ teaspoon pepper**

**1** In medium skillet over medium-high heat, heat oil. Add chicken and cook 8 minutes or until browned. Set chicken aside. Pour off fat.

**2** Add soup, milk, lemon juice and pepper. Heat to a boil. Return chicken to pan. Reduce heat to low. Cover and cook 5 minutes or until chicken is no longer pink.                    *Serves 4*

**Top to bottom: Asparagus & Ham Potato Topper and
Lemon Asparagus Chicken**

# EASY SKILLET BEEF & HASH BROWNS

**Prep/Cook Time:** 20 minutes    *20 minutes or less!*

> 1 pound ground beef
> 1 can (10¾ ounces) CAMPBELL'S Condensed Cream of
>     Celery Soup *or* 98% Fat Free Cream of Celery Soup
> ½ cup water
> ¼ cup ketchup
> 1 tablespoon Worcestershire sauce
> 2 cups frozen diced potatoes (hash browns)
> 3 slices process American cheese (about 3 ounces)

**1** In medium skillet over medium-high heat, cook beef until browned, stirring to separate meat. Pour off fat.

**2** Add soup, water, ketchup and Worcestershire. Heat to a boil. Stir in potatoes. Reduce heat to medium-low. Cover and cook 10 minutes or until potatoes are done, stirring occasionally. Top with cheese.                                        *Serves 4*

**Top to bottom: Quick Beef Skillet (page 98) and
Easy Skillet Beef & Hash Browns**

## QUICK BEEF SKILLET

*(photo on page 97)*

**Prep/Cook Time:** 15 minutes    *20 minutes or less!*

> 1 pound ground beef
> 1 can (10¾ ounces) CAMPBELL'S Condensed Tomato
>     Soup
> ¼ cup water
> 1 tablespoon Worcestershire sauce
> ¼ teaspoon pepper
> 1 can (about 15 ounces) sliced potatoes, drained
> 1 can (about 8 ounces) sliced carrots, drained

**1** In medium skillet over medium-high heat, cook beef until browned, stirring to separate meat. Pour off fat.

**2** Add soup, water, Worcestershire, pepper, potatoes and carrots. Reduce heat to low and heat through.         *Serves 4*

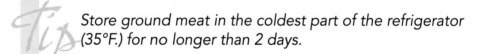

*Store ground meat in the coldest part of the refrigerator (35°F.) for no longer than 2 days.*

## ITALIAN BURGER MELT

*(photo on page 101)*

**Prep/Cook Time:** 20 minutes    *20 minutes or less!*

> 1 pound ground beef
> 1 can (11⅛ ounces) CAMPBELL'S Condensed Italian
>     Tomato Soup
> ¼ cup water
> 4 slices mozzarella, process American *or* Monterey Jack
>     cheese (about 4 ounces)
> 4 hamburger rolls, split and toasted

**1** Shape beef into 4 patties, ½ inch thick.

**2** In medium skillet over medium-high heat, cook patties until browned. Set patties aside. Pour off fat.

**3** Add soup and water. Heat to a boil. Return patties to pan. Reduce heat to low. Cover and cook 10 minutes or until patties are no longer pink (160°F.).

**4** Place cheese on patties and cook until cheese is melted. Place patties on 4 roll halves. Top with soup mixture and remaining roll halves.                                          *Makes 4 sandwiches*

**Serving Idea:** Serve with **Swanson Simple Seasoned Pasta.** In medium saucepan over medium-high heat, heat to a boil 2 cans (14½ ounces *each*) SWANSON Seasoned Chicken Broth with Italian Herbs. Stir in 3 cups *uncooked* corkscrew pasta. Reduce heat to medium. Simmer gently 10 minutes or until pasta is done, stirring occasionally. Serves about 6.

# FRENCH ONION BURGERS

*20 minutes or less!*

**1 pound ground beef**
**1 can (10½ ounces) CAMPBELL'S Condensed French**
**Onion Soup**
**4 round hard rolls, split**
**4 slices cheese (use your favorite)**

**1** Shape beef into 4 patties, ½ inch thick.

**2** In medium skillet over medium-high heat, cook patties until browned. Set patties aside. Pour off fat.

**3** Add soup. Heat to a boil. Return patties to pan. Reduce heat to low. Cover and cook 10 minutes or until patties are no longer pink (160°F.).

**4** Place cheese on patties and cook until cheese is melted. Place patties on 4 roll halves. Serve with soup mixture for dipping.

*Makes 4 sandwiches*

**Top to bottom: Italian Burger Melt (page 99) and
French Onion Burger**

# *Campbell's®*

# Speedy Skillets

## COUNTRY SKILLET SUPPER

**Prep Time:** 5 minutes    **Cook Time:** 25 minutes

    1 pound ground beef
    1 medium onion, chopped (about ½ cup)
   ⅛ teaspoon garlic powder *or* 1 clove garlic, minced
    1 can (10¾ ounces) CAMPBELL'S Condensed Golden
        Mushroom Soup
    1 can (10½ ounces) CAMPBELL'S Condensed Beef Broth
    1 can (14½ ounces) diced tomatoes
    1 small zucchini, sliced (about 1 cup)
   ½ teaspoon dried thyme leaves, crushed
  1½ cups *uncooked* corkscrew pasta

**1** In medium skillet over medium-high heat, cook beef, onion and garlic powder until beef is browned, stirring to separate meat. Pour off fat.

**2** Add soup, broth, tomatoes, zucchini and thyme. Heat to a boil. Stir in pasta. Reduce heat to low. Cook 15 minutes or until pasta is done, stirring often.                          *Serves 4*

**Country Skillet Supper Provençal:** Top with sliced pitted ripe olives.

**Country Skillet Supper**

# JAMBALAYA ONE DISH

**Prep Time:** 10 minutes     **Cook Time:**  20 minutes

    1 tablespoon vegetable oil
    ½ pound skinless, boneless chicken breasts, cut up
    ½ pound hot Italian pork sausage, sliced
    ¼ teaspoon garlic powder *or* 2 cloves garlic, minced
    1 can (10½ ounces) CAMPBELL'S Condensed French
        Onion Soup
    ⅓ cup PACE Picante Sauce *or* Thick & Chunky Salsa
    1 cup *uncooked* Minute® Original Rice
    ½ cup frozen peas
    ½ pound frozen cooked large shrimp

**1** In medium skillet over medium-high heat, heat oil. Add chicken, sausage and garlic powder and cook 5 minutes or until browned, stirring often. Pour off fat.

**2** Add soup and picante sauce. Heat to a boil. Stir in rice, peas and shrimp. Reduce heat to low. Cover and cook 5 minutes or until chicken and sausage are no longer pink and most of liquid is absorbed.                                          *Serves 4*

**Jambalaya One Dish**

# EASY BEEF & PASTA

*20 minutes or less!*

- **1 pound boneless beef sirloin steak, ¾ inch thick**
- **1 tablespoon vegetable oil**
- **1 can (10¾ ounces) CAMPBELL'S Condensed Tomato Soup**
- **½ cup water**
- **1 bag (about 16 ounces) frozen side dish seasoned pasta and vegetable combination**

**1** Slice beef into very thin strips.

**2** In medium skillet over medium-high heat, heat oil. Add beef and cook until beef is browned and juices evaporate, stirring often.

**3** Add soup, water and vegetable combination. Heat to a boil. Reduce heat to low. Cover and cook 5 minutes or until beef and vegetables are done, stirring occasionally.          *Serves 4*

 *For easier slicing, place beef in the freezer for 45 to 60 minutes or until it is partially frozen, then cut it into very thin slices.*

**Top to bottom: Chili Chicken Pasta Topper (page 113) and Easy Beef & Pasta**

# COUNTRY HERBED
# CHICKEN & VEGETABLES

**Prep Time:** 5 minutes    **Cook Time:** 25 minutes

1 tablespoon vegetable oil
1 pound skinless, boneless chicken breasts, cut up
1 can (10¾ ounces) CAMPBELL'S Condensed Cream of
    Chicken with Herbs Soup
½ cup milk
1 bag (16 ounces) frozen vegetable combination
    (broccoli, cauliflower, carrots)

**1** In medium skillet over medium-high heat, heat oil. Add chicken and cook until browned, stirring often. Set chicken aside. Pour off fat.

**2** Add soup, milk and vegetables. Heat to a boil. Return chicken to pan. Reduce heat to low. Cover and cook 10 minutes or until vegetables are tender.

*Serves 4*

*Tip* Substitute your favorite frozen vegetable combination for the broccoli, cauliflower and carrots combo called for here.

**Top to bottom: Herb Roasted Chicken & Potatoes (page141)
and Country Herbed Chicken & Vegetables**

# SHORTCUT STROGANOFF

**Prep Time:** 5 minutes      **Cook Time:**  30 minutes

> 1 pound boneless beef sirloin steak, ¾ inch thick
> 1 tablespoon vegetable oil
> 1 can (10¾ ounces) CAMPBELL'S Condensed Cream of
>     Mushroom Soup *or* 98% Fat Free Cream of
>     Mushroom Soup
> 1 can (10½ ounces) CAMPBELL'S Condensed Beef Broth
> 1 cup water
> 2 teaspoons Worcestershire sauce
> 3 cups *uncooked* corkscrew pasta
> ½ cup sour cream

**1** Slice beef into very thin strips.

**2** In medium skillet over medium-high heat, heat oil. Add beef and cook until beef is browned and juices evaporate, stirring often.

**3** Add soup, broth, water and Worcestershire. Heat to a boil. Stir in pasta. Reduce heat to medium. Cook 15 minutes or until pasta is done, stirring often. Stir in sour cream. Heat through.

*Serves 4*

**Top to bottom: Beef & Broccoli (page 112) and Shortcut Stroganoff**

# BEEF & BROCCOLI

*(photo on page 111)*

**Prep/Cook Time:** 25 minutes

> 1 pound boneless beef sirloin *or* top round steak, ¾ inch thick
> 1 tablespoon vegetable oil
> 1 can (10¾ ounces) CAMPBELL'S Condensed Tomato Soup
> 3 tablespoons soy sauce
> 1 tablespoon vinegar
> 1 teaspoon garlic powder
> ¼ teaspoon crushed red pepper (optional)
> 3 cups fresh *or* thawed frozen broccoli flowerets
> 4 cups hot cooked rice

**1** Slice beef into very thin strips.

**2** In medium skillet over medium-high heat, heat oil. Add beef and stir-fry until browned and juices evaporate.

**3** Add soup, soy sauce, vinegar, garlic powder and pepper. Heat to a boil. Reduce heat to medium. Add broccoli and cook until tender-crisp, stirring occasionally. Serve over rice. *Serves 4*

*Tip*  To thaw broccoli, microwave on HIGH 3 minutes.

# CHILI CHICKEN PASTA TOPPER

*(photo on page 107)*

**Prep/Cook Time:** 20 minutes     *20 minutes or less!*

1 tablespoon vegetable oil

1 pound skinless, boneless chicken breasts, cubed

1 can (10¾ ounces) CAMPBELL'S Condensed Cream of
   Chicken with Herbs Soup

½ cup milk

2 tablespoons grated Parmesan cheese

1 teaspoon chili powder

½ teaspoon garlic powder

4 cups hot cooked corkscrew pasta (about 3 cups
   uncooked)

**1** In medium skillet over medium-high heat, heat oil. Add chicken
and cook until browned, stirring often.

**2** Add soup, milk, cheese, chili powder and garlic powder and
cook through, stirring often. Serve over pasta.          *Serves 4*

*When a recipe will be served over pasta or rice,
save time by heating the cooking water while you're
preparing the recipe. It'll be ready when you are!*

# Campbell's

# Restaurant Style at Home

## EASY BEEF TERIYAKI

**Prep Time:** 10 minutes    **Cook Time:** 20 minutes

- 1 pound boneless beef sirloin steak, ¾ inch thick
- 1 tablespoon vegetable oil
- 1 can (10¾ ounces) CAMPBELL'S Condensed Golden Mushroom Soup
- 2 tablespoons soy sauce
- 1 tablespoon packed brown sugar
- 1 bag (about 16 ounces) frozen Oriental stir-fry vegetables
- 4 cups hot cooked rice

**1** Slice beef into very thin strips.

**2** In medium skillet over medium-high heat, heat oil. Add beef and stir-fry until beef is browned and juices evaporate.

**3** Add soup, soy sauce and sugar. Heat to a boil. Reduce heat to medium. Add vegetables. Cover and cook 5 minutes until vegetables are tender-crisp, stirring occasionally. Serve over rice.

*Serves 4*

**Top to bottom: Orange Beef (page 119) and Easy Beef Teriyaki**

# PAN ROASTED
# VEGETABLE & CHICKEN PIZZA

**Prep Time:** 20 minutes   **Cook Time:** 12 minutes

Vegetable cooking spray
¾ **pound skinless, boneless chicken breasts, cubed**
3 **cups cut-up vegetables***
⅛ **teaspoon garlic powder** *or* **1 clove garlic, minced**
1 **can (10¾ ounces) CAMPBELL'S Condensed Cream of Mushroom Soup** *or* **98% Fat Free Cream of Mushroom Soup**
1 **Italian bread shell (12-inch)**
1 **cup shredded Monterey Jack cheese (4 ounces)**

**1** Spray medium skillet with vegetable cooking spray and heat over medium-high heat 1 minute. Add chicken and cook 10 minutes or until browned, stirring often. Set chicken aside.

**2** Remove pan from heat. Spray with cooking spray. Reduce heat to medium. Add vegetables and garlic powder. Cook until tender-crisp. Add soup. Return chicken to pan. Heat through.

**3** Spread chicken mixture over shell to within ¼ inch of edge. Top with cheese. Bake at 450°F. for 12 minutes or until cheese is melted.                                              *Serves 4*

**\*Use a combination of sliced zucchini, red *or* green pepper cut into 2-inch long strips, and thinly sliced onion.**

**Top to bottom: Creamy Chicken Risotto (page 118)
and Pan Roasted Vegetable & Chicken Pizza**

# CREAMY CHICKEN RISOTTO

*(photo on page 117)*

**Prep Time:** 10 minutes     **Cook Time:** 35 minutes

    1 tablespoon vegetable oil
    1 pound skinless, boneless chicken breasts, cut up
    1 can (10¾ ounces) CAMPBELL'S Condensed Cream of
        Mushroom with Roasted Garlic Soup
    1 can (10½ ounces) CAMPBELL'S Condensed Chicken
        Broth
  ¾ cup water
    1 small carrot, shredded (about ⅓ cup)
    2 medium green onions, sliced (about ¼ cup)
    1 tablespoon grated Parmesan cheese
    1 cup *uncooked* regular long-grain white rice

**1** In medium skillet over medium-high heat, heat oil. Add chicken
and cook until browned, stirring often.

**2** Add soup, broth, water, carrot, onions and cheese. Heat to a
boil. Stir in rice. Reduce heat to low. Cover and cook 25 minutes
until chicken and rice are done and most of liquid is absorbed,
stirring occasionally.                                    *Serves 4*

## ORANGE BEEF

*(photo on page 115)*

**Prep Time:** 10 minutes    **Cook Time:** 20 minutes

**1 pound boneless beef sirloin steak, ¾ inch thick**
**2 tablespoons vegetable oil**
**1 medium green pepper, cut into 2-inch long strips**
   **(about 1½ cups)**
**1 medium onion, sliced (about ½ cup)**
**1 can (10¾ ounces) CAMPBELL'S Condensed Tomato**
   **Soup**
**¼ cup orange juice**
**2 tablespoons soy sauce**
**1 tablespoon vinegar**
**1 teaspoon garlic powder**
**4 cups hot cooked rice**

**1** Slice beef into very thin strips.

**2** In medium skillet over medium-high heat, heat *half* the oil. Add beef and stir-fry until beef is browned and juices evaporate.

**3** Reduce heat to medium. Add remaining oil. Add pepper and onion and cook until tender-crisp.

**4** Add soup, orange juice, soy sauce, vinegar and garlic powder. Heat through, stirring occasionally. Serve over rice.    *Serves 4*

# CHEESESTEAK POCKETS

**Prep/Cook Time:** 15 minutes    *20 minutes or less!*

  1 tablespoon vegetable oil
  1 medium onion, sliced (about ½ cup)
  1 package (14 ounces) frozen beef *or* chicken sandwich
    steaks, cut into 8 pieces
  1 can (10¾ ounces) CAMPBELL'S Condensed Cheddar
    Cheese Soup
  1 jar (about 4½ ounces) sliced mushrooms, drained
  4 pita breads (6-inch), cut in half, forming two pockets
    each

**1** In medium skillet over medium-high heat, heat oil. Add onion and cook until tender. Add sandwich steaks and cook 5 minutes or until browned, stirring often. Pour off fat.

**2** Add soup and mushrooms. Heat to a boil. Reduce heat to low and heat through. Spoon meat mixture into pita halves.

*Makes 4 sandwiches*

Top to bottom: Buffalo-Style Burger (page 122)
and Cheesesteak Pockets

# BUFFALO–STYLE BURGERS

*(photo on page 121)*

**Prep/Cook Time:** 20 minutes    *20 minutes or less!*

> 1 **pound ground beef**
> 1 **can (10¾ ounces) CAMPBELL'S Condensed Tomato Soup**
> ⅛ **teaspoon hot pepper sauce**
> 4 **hamburger rolls, split and toasted**
> ½ **cup crumbled blue cheese (about 4 ounces)**

**1** Shape beef into 4 patties, ½ inch thick.

**2** In medium skillet over medium-high heat, cook patties until browned. Set patties aside. Pour off fat.

**3** Add soup and hot pepper sauce. Heat to a boil. Return patties to pan. Reduce heat to low. Cover and cook 10 minutes or until patties are no longer pink (160°F.).

**4** Place patties on 4 roll halves. Top with cheese and remaining roll halves.

*Makes 4 sandwiches*

# MONTEREY CHICKEN FAJITAS

*(photo on page 125)*

**Prep Time:** 10 minutes     **Cook Time:** 20 minutes

2 tablespoons vegetable oil
1 pound skinless, boneless chicken breasts, cut into strips
1 medium green pepper, cut into 2-inch long strips
    (about 1½ cups)
1 medium onion, sliced (about ½ cup)
1 can (10¾ ounces) CAMPBELL'S Condensed Cream of
    Mushroom Soup *or* 98% Fat Free Cream of
    Mushroom Soup
½ cup PACE Thick & Chunky Salsa *or* Picante Sauce
8 flour tortillas (8-inch)
1 cup shredded Monterey Jack cheese (4 ounces)

**1** In medium skillet over medium-high heat, heat *half* the oil. Add chicken and cook until browned and juices evaporate, stirring often. Set chicken aside.

**2** Reduce heat to medium. Add remaining oil. Add pepper and onion and cook until tender-crisp. Pour off fat.

**3** Add soup and salsa. Heat to a boil. Return chicken to pan and heat through. Spoon *about ½ cup* chicken mixture down center of each tortilla. Top with cheese and additional salsa. Fold tortilla around filling.                                    *Serves 4*

# SOUTHWESTERN CHICKEN & PEPPER WRAPS

**Prep Time:** 10 minutes    **Cook/Stand Time:** 25 minutes

2 tablespoons vegetable oil
1 pound skinless, boneless chicken breasts, cut into strips
1 medium red pepper, cut into 2-inch long strips (about 1½ cups)
1 medium green pepper, cut into 2-inch long strips (about 1½ cups)
1 small onion, sliced (about ¼ cup)
1 can (10¾ ounces) CAMPBELL'S Condensed Golden Mushroom Soup
1 cup water
1 cup black beans, rinsed and drained (optional)
1 cup *uncooked* Minute® Original Rice
8 flour tortillas (8-inch)

1. In medium skillet over medium-high heat, heat **half** the oil. Add chicken and cook 10 minutes or until no longer pink and juices evaporate, stirring often.

2. Reduce heat to medium. Add remaining oil. Add peppers and onion and cook until tender-crisp, stirring often.

3. Add soup, water and beans. Heat to a boil. Stir in rice. Cover and remove from heat. Let stand 5 minutes.

4. Spoon ¾ **cup** chicken mixture down center of each tortilla. Fold tortilla around filling.

*Serves 4*

**Top to bottom: Monterey Chicken Fajita (page 123) and Southwestern Chicken & Pepper Wrap**

# Campbell's®

# Quick-Fix Oven Wonders

## ONE-DISH CHICKEN & RICE BAKE

**Prep Time:** 5 minutes     **Cook Time:** 45 minutes

    1 can (10¾ ounces) CAMPBELL'S Condensed Cream of Mushroom Soup *or* 98% Fat Free Cream of Mushroom Soup
    1 cup water*
    ¾ cup *uncooked* regular white rice
    ¼ teaspoon paprika
    ¼ teaspoon pepper
    4 skinless, boneless chicken breast halves (about 1 pound)

**1** In 2-quart shallow baking dish mix soup, water, rice, paprika and pepper. Place chicken on rice mixture. Sprinkle with additional paprika and pepper. **Cover.**

**2** Bake at 375°F. for 45 minutes or until chicken is no longer pink and rice is done.

*Serves 4*

*For creamier rice, increase water to 1⅓ cups.

**Top to bottom: One-Dish Chicken & Stuffing Bake (page 133) and One-Dish Chicken & Rice Bake**

# SIMPLY DELICIOUS MEAT LOAF

**Prep Time:** 5 minutes     **Cook Time:** 1 hour 5 minutes

>   1½ **pounds ground beef**
>    ½ **cup Italian-seasoned dry bread crumbs**
>    1 **egg, beaten**
>    1 **can (10¾ ounces) CAMPBELL'S Condensed Golden**
>       **Mushroom Soup**
>    ¼ **cup water**

**1** Mix beef, bread crumbs and egg *thoroughly*. In medium baking pan shape *firmly* into 8- by 4-inch loaf.

**2** Bake at 350°F. for 30 minutes. Spread ½ *can* soup over top of meat loaf. Bake 30 minutes more or until meat loaf is no longer pink (160°F.).

**3** In small saucepan mix *2 tablespoons* drippings, remaining soup and water. Heat through. Serve with meat loaf.          *Serves 6*

**Left to right: Parmesan Potatoes (page 151) and Simply Delicious Meat Loaf**

# FIESTA CHICKEN & RICE BAKE

**Prep Time:** 5 minutes    **Cook Time:** 45 minutes

  1 can (10¾ ounces) CAMPBELL'S Condensed Cream of
      Chicken Soup *or* 98% Fat Free Cream of Chicken
      Soup
  1 cup PACE Thick & Chunky Salsa *or* Picante Sauce
  ½ cup water
  1 cup whole kernel corn
  ¾ cup *uncooked* regular white rice
  4 skinless, boneless chicken breast halves (about
      1 pound)
      Paprika
  ½ cup shredded Cheddar cheese (2 ounces)

**1** In 2-quart shallow baking dish mix soup, salsa, water, corn
and rice. Place chicken on rice mixture. Sprinkle paprika over
chicken. **Cover**.

**2** Bake at 375°F. for 45 minutes or until chicken is no longer pink
and rice is done. Sprinkle with cheese.                    *Serves 4*

**Top to bottom: Asian Chicken & Rice Bake (page 132)
and Fiesta Chicken & Rice Bake**

# ASIAN CHICKEN & RICE BAKE

*(photo on page 131)*

**Prep Time:** 5 minutes    **Cook Time:** 45 minutes

    ¾ cup *uncooked* regular white rice
    4 skinless, boneless chicken breast halves (about
        1 pound)
    1 can (10¾ ounces) CAMPBELL'S Condensed Golden
        Mushroom Soup
    ¾ cup water
    2 tablespoons soy sauce
    2 tablespoons cider vinegar
    2 tablespoons honey
    1 teaspoon garlic powder
        Paprika

**1** Spread rice in 2-quart shallow baking dish. Place chicken on rice.

**2** Mix soup, water, soy sauce, vinegar, honey and garlic powder. Pour over chicken. Sprinkle with paprika. **Cover**.

**3** Bake at 375°F. for 45 minutes or until chicken is no longer pink and rice is done.

*Serves 4*

**Sesame Asian Chicken & Rice Bake:** Sprinkle with toasted sesame seeds after baking.

# ONE–DISH CHICKEN & STUFFING BAKE

*(photo on page 127)*

**Prep Time:** 10 minutes    **Cook Time:** 30 minutes

> 1¼ cups boiling water
> 4 tablespoons margarine *or* butter, melted
> 4 cups PEPPERIDGE FARM Herb Seasoned Stuffing
> 4 to 6 skinless, boneless chicken breast halves (about 1 to 1½ pounds)
> Paprika
> 1 can (10¾ ounces) CAMPBELL'S Condensed Cream of Mushroom Soup *or* 98% Fat Free Cream of Mushroom Soup
> ⅓ cup milk
> 1 tablespoon chopped fresh parsley *or* 1 teaspoon dried parsley flakes

**1** Mix water and margarine. Add stuffing. Mix lightly.

**2** Spoon stuffing across center of 3-quart shallow baking dish, leaving space on both sides for chicken. Arrange chicken on each side of stuffing. Sprinkle paprika over chicken.

**3** Mix soup, milk and parsley. Pour over chicken.

**4** **Cover.** Bake at 400°F. for 30 minutes or until chicken is no longer pink.                                    *Serves 4 to 6*

# GARLIC MASHED POTATOES & BEEF BAKE

**Prep Time:** 10 minutes    **Cook Time:** 20 minutes

1 pound ground beef
1 can (10¾ ounces) CAMPBELL'S Condensed Cream of
    Mushroom with Roasted Garlic Soup
1 tablespoon Worcestershire sauce
1 bag (16 ounces) frozen vegetable combination
    (broccoli, cauliflower, carrots), thawed
3 cups hot mashed potatoes

**1** In medium skillet over medium-high heat, cook beef until browned, stirring to separate meat. Pour off fat.

**2** In 2-quart shallow baking dish mix beef, *½ **can*** soup, Worcestershire and vegetables.

**3** Stir remaining soup into potatoes. Spoon potato mixture over beef mixture. Bake at 400°F. for 20 minutes or until hot.

*Serves 4*

*Tip* | To thaw vegetables, microwave on HIGH 3 minutes.

**Garlic Mashed Potatoes & Beef Bake**

# HAM & BROCCOLI
# SHORTCUT STROMBOLI

**Prep Time:** 10 minutes     **Cook Time:** 20 minutes

- **1 package (10 ounces) refrigerated pizza dough**
- **1 can (10¾ ounces) CAMPBELL'S Condensed Cream of Celery Soup**
- **1 cup cooked chopped broccoli**
- **2 cups cubed cooked ham**
- **1 cup shredded Cheddar cheese (4 ounces)**

**1** Preheat oven to 400°F. Unroll dough onto greased baking sheet. Set aside.

**2** Mix soup, broccoli and ham. Spread soup mixture down center of dough. Top with cheese. Fold long sides of dough over filling and pinch and seal. Pinch short sides to seal.

**3** Bake 20 minutes or until golden brown. Slice and serve.

*Serves 4*

**Roast Beef & Bean Shortcut Stromboli:** Substitute 1 can CAMPBELL'S Condensed Cream of Mushroom Soup, 1 cup cut green beans and 2 cups cubed cooked roast beef for Cream of Celery Soup, broccoli and ham.

**Chicken & Vegetable Shortcut Stromboli:** Substitute 1 can CAMPBELL'S Condensed Cream of Chicken Soup, 1 cup mixed vegetables and 2 cups cubed cooked chicken *or* turkey for Cream of Celery Soup, broccoli and ham.

**Top to bottom: Cod Vera Cruz (page 140) and Ham & Broccoli Shortcut Stromboli**

## E-Z CHICKEN TORTILLA BAKE

**Prep Time:** 10 minutes     **Cook Time:** 30 minutes

1 can (10¾ ounces) CAMPBELL'S Condensed Tomato Soup
1 cup PACE Thick & Chunky Salsa *or* Picante Sauce
½ cup milk
2 cups cubed cooked chicken *or* turkey
8 corn tortillas (6- *or* 8-inch), cut into 1-inch pieces
1 cup shredded Cheddar cheese (4 ounces)

**1** In 2-quart shallow baking dish mix soup, salsa, milk, chicken, tortillas and *half* the cheese. **Cover.**

**2** Bake at 400°F. for 30 minutes or until hot. Top with remaining cheese.

*Serves 4*

## SLOPPY JOE PIZZA

**Prep Time:** 10 minutes     **Cook Time:** 12 minutes

¾ pound ground beef
1 can (10¾ ounces) CAMPBELL'S Condensed Tomato Soup
1 Italian bread shell (12-inch)
1½ cups shredded Cheddar cheese (6 ounces)

**1** In medium skillet over medium-high heat, cook beef until browned, stirring to separate meat. Pour off fat.

**2** Add soup. Heat through. Spread beef mixture over shell to within ¼ inch of edge. Top with cheese. Bake at 450°F. for 12 minutes or until cheese is melted.

*Serves 4*

**Top to bottom: E-Z Chicken Tortilla Bake, 3-Cheese Pasta Bake (page 140) and Sloppy Joe Pizza**

## COD VERA CRUZ

*(photo on page 137)*

**Prep Time:** 10 minutes    **Cook Time:** 20 minutes

  1 pound fresh *or* thawed frozen cod *or* haddock fillets
  1 can (10¾ ounces) CAMPBELL'S Condensed Tomato Soup
  1 can (10½ ounces) CAMPBELL'S Condensed Chicken Broth
  ⅓ cup PACE Thick & Chunky Salsa *or* Picante Sauce
  1 tablespoon lime juice
  2 teaspoons chopped fresh cilantro
  1 teaspoon dried oregano leaves, crushed
  ⅛ teaspoon garlic powder *or* 1 clove garlic, minced
  4 cups hot cooked rice

**1** Place fish in 2-quart shallow baking dish.

**2** Mix soup, broth, salsa, lime juice, cilantro, oregano and garlic powder. Pour over fish. Bake at 400°F. for 20 minutes or until fish flakes easily when tested with a fork. Serve over rice.

*Serves 4*

## 3-CHEESE PASTA BAKE

*(photo on page 139)*

**Prep Time:** 10 minutes    **Cook Time:** 20 minutes

  1 can (10¾ ounces) CAMPBELL'S Condensed Cream of
      Mushroom Soup *or* 98% Fat Free Cream of
      Mushroom Soup
  1 package (8 ounces) shredded 2-cheese blend (2 cups)
  ⅓ cup grated Parmesan cheese
  1 cup milk
  ¼ teaspoon pepper
  4 cups cooked corkscrew pasta (about 3 cups uncooked)

In 1½-quart casserole mix soup, cheeses, milk and pepper. Stir in pasta. Bake at 400°F. for 20 minutes or until hot.    *Serves 4*

# HERB ROASTED CHICKEN & POTATOES

*(photo on page 109)*

**Prep Time:** 10 minutes    **Cook Time:** 30 minutes

    1 large plastic oven bag
    4 skinless, boneless chicken breast halves (about
        1 pound)
    8 small red potatoes, cut into quarters (about 1 pound)
    1 can (10¾ ounces) CAMPBELL'S Condensed Cream of
        Chicken with Herbs Soup
    ¼ cup water
    ½ teaspoon garlic powder
      Chopped fresh parsley for garnish

**1** Preheat oven to 375°F. Prepare oven bag according to package directions using *1 tablespoon all-purpose flour.* Place chicken and potatoes in oven bag.

**2** In a small bowl mix soup, water and garlic powder. Pour into oven bag. Close bag with nylon tie. Cut 6 (½-inch) slits in top of bag.

**3** Bake at 375°F. for 30 minutes or until chicken is no longer pink and potatoes are done. Garnish with parsley.          *Serves 4*

> *Tip* *Coating the inside of the oven bag with flour protects it from bursting during baking.*

# FLASH ROASTED
# CRISPY RANCH CHICKEN

**Prep Time:** 5 minutes     **Cook Time:** 20 minutes

1 can (10¾ ounces) CAMPBELL'S Condensed Cream of
   Chicken Soup *or* 98% Fat Free Cream of Chicken
   Soup
½ cup milk
1 envelope (1 ounce) ranch salad dressing mix
4 skinless, boneless chicken breast halves (about
   1 pound)
1½ cups finely crushed tortilla chips
2 tablespoons margarine *or* butter, melted

**1** In shallow dish mix soup, milk and dressing mix. Reserve *1 cup* for sauce.

**2** Dip chicken into soup mixture. Coat with tortilla chips.

**3** Place chicken on greased baking sheet. Drizzle with margarine. Bake at 400°F. for 20 minutes or until chicken is no longer pink.

**4** In small saucepan over medium heat, heat reserved soup mixture to a boil. Serve with chicken.                    *Serves 4*

Left to right: Creamy Vegetable Medley (page 194)
and Flash Roasted Crispy Ranch Chicken

# CORNBREAD CHICKEN POT PIE

**Prep Time:** 10 minutes   **Cook Time:** 30 minutes

1 can (10¾ ounces) CAMPBELL'S Condensed Cream of
  Chicken Soup *or* 98% Fat Free Cream of Chicken
  Soup
1 can (about 8 ounces) whole kernel corn, drained
2 cups cubed cooked chicken *or* turkey
1 package (8½ ounces) corn muffin mix
¾ cup milk
1 egg
½ cup shredded Cheddar cheese (2 ounces)

**1** Preheat oven to 400°F. In 9-inch pie plate mix soup, corn and chicken.

**2** Mix muffin mix, milk and egg. Pour over chicken mixture. Bake for 30 minutes or until golden. Sprinkle with cheese.

*Serves 4*

**Cornbread Chicken Chili Pot Pie:** In Step 1 add 1 can (about 4 ounces) chopped green chilies, drained, with the corn.

*Don't waste time shredding or grating cheese. Buy packaged shredded/grated cheese at the store. You'll save at least 5 minutes, and you won't have to clean the grater!*

**Cornbread Chicken Pot Pie**

# *Campbell's*

# Simple Sides

## CHEDDARY POUCH POTATOES

**Prep Time:** 5 minutes     **Cook Time:** 25 minutes

> 1 can (10¾ ounces) CAMPBELL'S Condensed Cheddar
>    Cheese Soup
> ¼ cup milk
> ½ teaspoon garlic powder
> ¼ teaspoon onion powder
> 4 cups frozen steak fries
>    Paprika

**1** In large bowl mix soup, milk, garlic powder and onion powder. Stir in potatoes.

**2** Cut four 14-inch squares of heavy-duty aluminum foil. Spoon *1 cup* soup mixture onto each square, arranging potatoes to make a single layer. Sprinkle with paprika. Bring up sides of foil and double fold. Double fold ends to make packet.

**3** Place potato packets on grill rack over medium-hot coals. Grill 25 minutes or until potatoes are tender.          *Serves 4*

**Cheddary Oven Pouch Potatoes:** In Step 3, on baking sheet bake packets at 350°F. for 25 minutes.

Top to bottom: Cheddar Broccoli Bake
(page 150) and Cheddary Pouch Potatoes

## CHEESY BROCCOLI

**Prep/Cook Time:** 10 minutes    *20 minutes or less!*

    **1 can (10¾ ounces) CAMPBELL'S Condensed Cheddar
       Cheese Soup
    ¼ cup milk
    4 cups frozen broccoli cuts**

**1** In 2-quart microwave-safe casserole mix soup and milk. Add broccoli.

**2** Cover and microwave on HIGH 8 minutes or until broccoli is tender-crisp, stirring once during heating.    *Serves 4*

## CHEESE FRIES

**Prep/Cook Time:** 20 minutes    *20 minutes or less!*

    **1 bag (32 ounces) frozen French fried potatoes
    1 can (10¾ ounces) CAMPBELL'S Condensed Cheddar
       Cheese Soup**

**1** On baking sheet bake potatoes according to package directions.

**2** Push potatoes into pile in center of baking sheet. Stir soup in can and spoon over potatoes.

**3** Bake 3 minutes more or until soup is hot.    *Serves 6*

**Nacho Cheese Fries:** Substitute CAMPBELL'S Condensed Fiesta Nacho Cheese Soup for the Cheddar Cheese Soup.

**Top to bottom: Cheese Fries and
Cheesy Broccoli**

# CHEDDAR BROCCOLI BAKE

*(photo on page 147)*

**Prep Time:** 10 minutes    **Cook Time:** 30 minutes

- 1 can (10¾ ounces) CAMPBELL'S Condensed Cheddar Cheese Soup
- ½ cup milk
  Dash pepper
- 4 cups cooked broccoli cuts
- 1 can (2.8 ounces) French's® French Fried Onions (1⅓ cups)

**1** In 1½-quart casserole mix soup, milk, pepper, broccoli and ½ *can* onions.

**2** Bake at 350°F. for 25 minutes or until hot.

**3** Stir. Sprinkle remaining onions over broccoli mixture. Bake 5 minutes more or until onions are golden.    *Serves 6*

*Tip*  *Two pounds of fresh broccoli will yield 4 cups broccoli cuts.*

# PARMESAN POTATOES

*(photo on page 129)*

**Prep Time:** 5 minutes    **Cook Time:** 45 minutes

> 1 can (10¾ ounces) CAMPBELL'S Condensed Cheddar
>     Cheese Soup
> ½ cup milk
> ½ cup grated Parmesan cheese
> ¼ teaspoon pepper
> 4 medium white potatoes, cut into 1-inch pieces (about
>     4 cups)
> 1 can (2.8 ounces) French's® French Fried Onions
>     (1⅓ cups)

**1** In greased shallow 2-quart baking dish mix soup, milk, cheese and pepper. Stir in potatoes and ½ **can** onions.

**2** Bake at 400°F. for 40 minutes or until potatoes are tender. Sprinkle remaining onions over potatoes. Bake 5 minutes more or until onions are golden.

*Serves 4*

# Campbell's®

# Slow Cooker Creations

## GOLDEN MUSHROOM PORK & APPLES

**Prep Time:** 10 minutes     **Cook Time:**  8 to 9 hours

> 2 cans (10¾ ounces *each*) CAMPBELL'S Condensed
>     Golden Mushroom Soup
> ½ cup water
> 1 tablespoon brown sugar
> 1 tablespoon Worcestershire sauce
> 1 teaspoon dried thyme leaves, crushed
> 4 large Granny Smith apples, sliced (about 4 cups)
> 2 large onions, sliced (about 2 cups)
> 8 boneless pork chops, ¾ inch thick (about 2 pounds)

In slow cooker mix soup, water, brown sugar, Worcestershire and thyme. Add apples, onions and pork. Cover and cook on **low** 8 to 9 hours or until pork is tender.          *Serves 8*

**Top to bottom: Savory Pot Roast (page 157) and Golden Mushroom Pork & Apples**

# LEMON CHICKEN

**Prep Time:** 5 minutes     **Cook Time:** 7 to 8 hours

> 2 cans (10¾ ounces *each*) CAMPBELL'S Condensed Cream of Chicken Soup *or* 98% Fat Free Cream of Chicken Soup
> ½ cup water
> ¼ cup lemon juice
> 2 teaspoons Dijon-style mustard
> 1½ teaspoons garlic powder
> 8 large carrots, thickly sliced (about 6 cups)
> 8 skinless, boneless chicken breast halves (about 2 pounds)
> 8 cups hot cooked egg noodles
> Grated Parmesan cheese

**1** In slow cooker mix soup, water, lemon juice, mustard, garlic powder and carrots. Add chicken and turn to coat. Cover and cook on **low** 7 to 8 hours or until chicken is done.

**2** Serve over noodles. Sprinkle with cheese.          *Serves 8*

**Top to bottom: Asian Tomato Beef (page 156) and Lemon Chicken**

# ASIAN TOMATO BEEF

*(photo on page 155)*

**Prep Time:** 10 minutes     **Cook Time:** 7 to 8 hours and
15 minutes

     2 cans (10¾ ounces *each*) CAMPBELL'S Condensed
          Tomato Soup
     ⅓ cup soy sauce
     ⅓ cup vinegar
     1½ teaspoons garlic powder
     ¼ teaspoon pepper
     1 (3- to 3½-pound) boneless beef round steak, ¾ inch
          thick, cut into strips
     6 cups broccoli flowerets
     8 cups hot cooked rice

**1** In slow cooker mix soup, soy sauce, vinegar, garlic powder,
pepper and beef. Cover and cook on **low** 7 to 8 hours or until
beef is done.

**2** Stir. Arrange broccoli over beef. Cover and cook on **high**
15 minutes more or until tender-crisp. Serve over rice.

*Serves 8*

*No time to chop fresh produce? Buy bags of precut
vegetables—they work great in many recipes!*

# SAVORY POT ROAST

*(photo on page 153)*

**Prep Time:** 10 minutes    **Cook Time:** 8 to 9 hours

- 1 can (10¾ ounces) CAMPBELL'S Condensed Cream of Mushroom Soup *or* 98% Fat Free Cream of Mushroom Soup
- 1 pouch CAMPBELL'S Dry Onion Soup and Recipe Mix
- 6 medium potatoes, cut into 1-inch pieces (about 6 cups)
- 6 medium carrots, thickly sliced (about 3 cups)
- 1 (3½- to 4-pound) boneless chuck pot roast, trimmed

In slow cooker mix soup, soup mix, potatoes and carrots. Add roast and turn to coat. Cover and cook on *low* 8 to 9 hours or until roast and vegetables are done.                    *Serves 7 to 8*

# NACHO CHICKEN & RICE WRAPS

**Prep Time:** 5 minutes     **Cook Time:** 7 to 8 hours

2 cans (10¾ ounces *each*) CAMPBELL'S Condensed Cheddar Cheese Soup
1 cup water
2 cups PACE Thick & Chunky Salsa *or* Picante Sauce
1¼ cups *uncooked* regular long-grain white rice
2 pounds skinless, boneless chicken breasts, cut into cubes
10 flour tortillas (10-inch)

**1** In slow cooker mix soup, water, salsa, rice and chicken. Cover and cook on **low** 7 to 8 hours or until chicken and rice are done.

**2** Spoon **about 1 cup** rice mixture down center of each tortilla.

**3** Fold opposite sides of tortilla over filling. Roll up from bottom. Cut each wrap in half.                    *Serves 10*

*Tip*  For firmer rice, substitute converted rice for regular.

For information on purchasing the *Campbell's* Slow Cooker, please call 1-888-768-7766.

**Top to bottom: Creamy Chicken & Wild Rice (page 160) and Nacho Chicken & Rice Wrap**

# CREAMY CHICKEN & WILD RICE

*(photo on page 159)*

**Prep Time:** 5 minutes    **Cook Time:** 7 to 8 hours

2 cans (10¾ ounces *each*) CAMPBELL'S Condensed Cream of Chicken Soup *or* 98% Fat Free Cream of Chicken Soup

1½ cups water

1 package (6 ounces) seasoned long-grain and wild rice mix

4 large carrots, thickly sliced (about 3 cups)

8 skinless, boneless chicken breast halves (about 2 pounds)

In slow cooker mix soup, water, rice and carrots. Add chicken and turn to coat. Cover and cook on **low** 7 to 8 hours or until chicken and rice are done.                  *Serves 8*

# Campbell's®

# CLASSIC
## RECIPES

# Campbell's

# CLASSIC
## RECIPES

# Campbell's
# APPETIZERS & SWEETS

## Stuffed Clams

**Prep Time:** 35 minutes    **Cook Time:** 20 minutes

24 cherrystone clams, scrubbed
2 slices bacon, diced
3 tablespoons margarine *or* butter
1 medium onion, chopped (about ½ cup)
¼ teaspoon garlic powder *or* 2 cloves garlic, minced
1½ cups PEPPERIDGE FARM Herb Seasoned Stuffing
2 tablespoons grated Parmesan cheese
2 tablespoons chopped fresh parsley *or* 2 teaspoons dried parsley flakes

**1.** Open clams. Remove and discard top shell. Arrange clams in large shallow baking pan.

**2.** In medium skillet over medium heat, cook bacon until crisp. Remove and drain on paper towels.

**3.** Add margarine, onion and garlic powder to hot drippings and cook until tender. Add stuffing, cheese, parsley and bacon. Mix lightly. Spoon on top of each clam. Bake at 400°F. for 20 minutes or until clams are done.          *Makes 24 appetizers*

Clockwise from top left: *Sausage Stuffed Mushrooms (page 164),*
*Stuffed Clams and Savory Criss-Cross Pastry (page 169)*

# Sausage Stuffed Mushrooms

*(photo on page 163)*
**Prep Time:** 25 minutes    **Cook Time:** 10 minutes

24 medium mushrooms (about 1 pound)
2 tablespoons margarine *or* butter, melted
¼ pound bulk pork sausage
1 cup PACE Picante Sauce *or* Thick & Chunky Salsa
½ cup dry bread crumbs
Chopped fresh cilantro *or* parsley

1. Remove stems from mushrooms. Chop enough stems to make *1 cup* and set aside. Brush mushroom caps with margarine and place top-side down in shallow baking pan. Set aside.

2. In medium skillet over medium-high heat, cook sausage and chopped mushroom stems until sausage is browned, stirring to separate meat.

3. Add ½ *cup* picante sauce and bread crumbs. Mix lightly. Spoon about *1 tablespoon* stuffing mixture into each mushroom cap.

4. Bake at 425°F. for 10 minutes or until mushrooms are heated through. Top each with *1 teaspoon* remaining picante sauce and cilantro.                        *Makes 24 appetizers*

*Tip*

To make ahead, prepare through step 3. Cover and refrigerate up to 24 hours. Bake as in step 4.

# Spinach-Cheese Swirls

*(photo on page 167)*
**Thaw Time:** 30 minutes
**Prep Time:** 20 minutes     **Cook Time:** 15 minutes

½ package (17¼-ounce size) **PEPPERIDGE FARM**
    **Frozen Puff Pastry Sheets (1 sheet)**
1 **egg**
1 **tablespoon water**
½ **cup shredded Muenster** *or* **Monterey Jack cheese**
    **(2 ounces)**
¼ **cup grated Parmesan cheese**
1 **green onion, chopped (about 2 tablespoons)**
⅛ **teaspoon garlic powder**
1 **package (about 10 ounces) frozen chopped**
    **spinach, thawed and** *well drained*

**1.** Thaw pastry sheet at room temperature 30 minutes. Preheat oven to 400°F. Mix egg and water and set aside. Mix Muenster cheese, Parmesan cheese, onion and garlic powder. Set aside.

**2.** Unfold pastry on lightly floured surface. Brush with egg mixture. Top with cheese mixture and spinach. Starting at one side, roll up like a jelly roll. Cut into 20 (½-inch) slices. Place 2 inches apart on baking sheet. Brush tops with egg mixture.

**3.** Bake 15 minutes or until golden.                    *Makes 20 appetizers*

To thaw spinach, microwave on HIGH 3 minutes, breaking apart with fork halfway through heating.

# Ham and Broccoli Swirls

**Thaw Time:** 30 minutes
**Prep Time:** 20 minutes    **Cook Time:** 15 minutes

½ package (17¼-ounce size) PEPPERIDGE FARM
   Frozen Puff Pastry Sheets (1 sheet)
1 egg
1 tablespoon water
1 container (4 ounces) whipped cream cheese with
   chives spread
1 package (10 ounces) frozen chopped broccoli
   (2 cups), thawed and *well drained*
1 cup finely chopped cooked ham

**1.** Thaw pastry sheet at room temperature 30 minutes. Preheat oven to 400°F. Mix egg and water and set aside.

**2.** Unfold pastry on lightly floured surface. Roll into 16- by 12-inch rectangle. Spread cream cheese over rectangle to within ½ inch of edges. Top with broccoli and ham. Starting at long side, roll up like a jelly roll, only to center. Roll up opposite side to center. Brush between rolls with egg mixture, then gently press rolls together.

**3.** Cut into 32 (½-inch) slices. Place 2 inches apart on greased baking sheet. Brush tops with egg mixture.

**4.** Bake 15 minutes or until golden. Serve warm or at room temperature.                               *Makes 32 appetizers*

*Tip*

To make ahead, prepare through step 3. Freeze. When frozen, store in plastic bag up to 1 month. To bake, preheat oven to 400°F. Place frozen slices on baking sheet. Bake 20 minutes or until golden.

Clockwise from top: *Parmesan Cheese Crisps (page 168),
Spinach-Cheese Swirls (page 165) and Ham and Broccoli Swirls*

# Parmesan Cheese Crisps

*(photo on page 167)*
**Thaw Time:** 30 minutes
**Prep Time:** 20 minutes     **Cook Time:** 10 minutes

   ½ **package (17¼-ounce size) PEPPERIDGE FARM**
       **Frozen Puff Pastry Sheets (1 sheet)**
   1 **egg**
   1 **tablespoon water**
   ¼ **cup grated Parmesan cheese**
   1 **tablespoon chopped fresh parsley *or* 1 teaspoon**
       **dried parsley flakes**
   ½ **teaspoon dried oregano leaves, crushed**

**1.** Thaw pastry sheet at room temperature 30 minutes. Preheat oven to 400°F. Mix egg and water and set aside. Mix cheese, parsley and oregano and set aside.

**2.** Unfold pastry on lightly floured surface. Roll into 14- by 10-inch rectangle. Cut in half lengthwise. Brush both halves with egg mixture. Top 1 rectangle with cheese mixture. Place remaining rectangle over cheese-topped rectangle, egg-side down. Roll gently with rolling pin to seal.

**3.** Cut crosswise into 28 (½-inch) strips. Twist strips and place 2 inches apart on greased baking sheet, pressing down ends. Brush with egg mixture.

**4.** Bake 10 minutes or until golden. Serve warm or at room temperature.      *Makes 28 appetizers*

*Tip*

To make ahead, twist strips. Place on baking sheet and brush with egg mixture. Freeze. When frozen, store in plastic bag for up to 1 month. To bake, preheat oven to 400°F. Place frozen strips on greased baking sheet. Bake 15 minutes or until golden.

# Savory Criss-Cross Pastry

*(photo on page 163)*
**Thaw Time:** 30 minutes
**Prep Time:** 20 minutes    **Cook Time:** 35 minutes

½ package (17¼-ounce size) **PEPPERIDGE FARM**
  **Frozen Puff Pastry Sheets (1 sheet)**
2 **eggs**
1 **tablespoon water**
½ **pound bulk pork sausage**
1 **cup PEPPERIDGE FARM Herb Seasoned Stuffing**
1 **small onion, chopped (about ¼ cup)**
1 **cup chopped mushrooms (about 3 ounces)**

**1.** Thaw pastry sheet at room temperature 30 minutes. Preheat oven to 375°F. Mix **1** egg and water and set aside.

**2.** Mix sausage, stuffing, remaining egg, onion and mushrooms *thoroughly.*

**3.** Unfold pastry on lightly floured surface. Cut slits 1 inch apart from outer edge up to fold mark on each side of pastry. Spoon sausage mixture down center of pastry. Starting at one end, fold pastry strips over stuffing mixture, alternating sides, to cover sausage mixture. Place on baking sheet. Brush with egg mixture.

**4.** Bake 35 minutes or until golden. Slice and serve warm.

*Serves 4 as a main dish or 8 as an appetizer*

# Caramel Apple Tarts

**Thaw Time:** 30 minutes
**Prep Time:** 20 minutes     **Cook Time:** 25 minutes

1 package (10 ounces) PEPPERIDGE FARM Frozen
   Puff Pastry Shells
6 tablespoons sugar
½ teaspoon ground cinnamon
½ teaspoon ground ginger
3 apples *or* pears, peeled, cored and thinly sliced
   (about 4 cups)
⅔ cup caramel sauce
   Vanilla ice cream

**1.** Thaw pastry shells at room temperature 30 minutes. Preheat oven to 375°F. Mix sugar, cinnamon and ginger and set aside.

**2.** Roll pastry shells into 5-inch circles on lightly floured surface. Place on 2 shallow-sided baking sheets. Divide apple slices among pastry circles. Sprinkle each with **1 tablespoon** sugar mixture. Bake 25 minutes or until pastry is golden.

**3.** In small saucepan over medium heat, heat caramel sauce until warm. Spoon over tarts. Serve with ice cream.     *Serves 6*

*Tip*

For more delicious PEPPERIDGE FARM Puff Pastry
recipes and ideas, visit our Web site at
www.puffpastry.com

Left to right: *Caramel Apple Tarts
and Apple Strudel (page 175)*

# Lemon Meringue Tarts

**Bake Time:** 30 minutes

**Prep Time:** 20 minutes    **Cook Time:** 15 minutes

> 1 package (10 ounces) PEPPERIDGE FARM Frozen Puff Pastry Shells
> 1 package (3 ounces) lemon pudding mix
> 1 teaspoon grated lemon peel
> 2 egg whites
> ¼ cup sugar

**1.** Bake and cool pastry shells according to package directions.

**2.** Prepare pudding mix according to package directions for pie filling. Stir in lemon peel and cool to room temperature.

**3.** Spoon about ⅓ *cup* pudding into each pastry shell. Preheat oven to 325°F.

**4.** In medium bowl place egg whites. Beat with electric mixer at high speed until frothy. Gradually add sugar, beating until soft peaks form. Spoon over pudding sealing edges. Place on baking sheet. Bake 12 minutes or until lightly browned. Remove from baking sheet and cool on wire rack.

*Serves 6*

**Variation:** Substitute sweetened whipped cream *or* whipped topping for egg whites and sugar. Top each filled pastry shell with whipped cream. Garnish with lemon slices if desired. Serve immediately or cover and refrigerate until serving time.

Top to bottom: *Southern Pecan Crisps (page 174) and Lemon Meringue Tarts*

# Southern Pecan Crisps

*(photo on page 173)*
**Thaw Time:** 30 minutes
**Prep Time:** 25 minutes    **Cook Time:** 12 minutes

½ package (17¼-ounce size) PEPPERIDGE FARM
   Frozen Puff Pastry Sheets (1 sheet)
½ cup packed brown sugar
2 tablespoons margarine *or* butter, melted
⅓ cup chopped pecans
   Confectioners' sugar

**1.** Thaw pastry sheet at room temperature 30 minutes. Preheat oven to 400°F. Mix brown sugar, margarine and pecans and set aside.

**2.** Unfold pastry on lightly floured surface. Roll into 15- by 12-inch rectangle. Cut into 20 (3-inch) squares. Press squares into bottoms of 3-inch muffin-pan cups. Place **1 heaping teaspoon** pecan mixture in center of each.

**3.** Bake 12 minutes or until golden. Remove from pans. Cool on wire rack. Sprinkle with confectioners' sugar.

*Makes 20 pastries*

*Tip*

Wrap unused pastry sheets in plastic wrap or foil and return to the freezer. Thawed pastry sheets will be cool to the touch and will unfold without breaking. Thawed pastry sheets can be refrigerated up to 2 days.

# Apple Strudel

*(photo on page 171)*
**Thaw Time:** 30 minutes
**Prep Time:** 30 minutes    **Cook Time:** 35 minutes

½ package (17¼-ounce size) **PEPPERIDGE FARM Frozen Puff Pastry Sheets (1 sheet)**
1 egg
1 tablespoon water
2 tablespoons sugar
1 tablespoon all-purpose flour
¼ teaspoon ground cinnamon
2 large Granny Smith apples, peeled, cored and thinly sliced (about 3 cups)
2 tablespoons raisins

**1.** Thaw pastry sheet at room temperature 30 minutes. Preheat oven to 375°F. Mix egg and water and set aside. Mix sugar, flour and cinnamon. Add apples and raisins and toss to coat. Set aside.

**2.** Unfold pastry on lightly floured surface. Roll into 16- by 12-inch rectangle. With short side facing you, spoon apple mixture on bottom half of pastry to within 1 inch of edges. Starting at short side, roll up like a jelly roll. Place seam-side down on baking sheet. Tuck ends under to seal. Brush with egg mixture. Cut several 2-inch-long slits 2 inches apart on top.

**3.** Bake 35 minutes or until golden. Cool on baking sheet on wire rack 30 minutes. Slice and serve warm. Sprinkle with confectioners' sugar if desired.

*Serves 6*

**Variation:** Omit raisins.

# Chocolate Mousse Napoleons with Strawberries & Cream

**Thaw Time:** 30 minutes
**Prep Time:** 25 minutes    **Cook Time:** 15 minutes

½ package (17¼-ounce size) PEPPERIDGE FARM
  Frozen Puff Pastry Sheets (1 sheet)
1 cup heavy cream
¼ teaspoon ground cinnamon
1 package (6 ounces) semi-sweet chocolate pieces,
  melted and cooled
2 cups sweetened whipped cream *or* whipped
  topping
1½ cups sliced strawberries
1 square (1 ounce) semi-sweet chocolate, melted
  (optional)
Confectioners' sugar

1. Thaw pastry sheet at room temperature 30 minutes. Preheat oven to 400°F.

2. Unfold pastry on lightly floured surface. Cut into 3 strips along fold marks. Cut each strip into 6 rectangles.

3. Bake 15 minutes or until golden. Remove from baking sheet and cool on wire rack.

4. In medium bowl place cream and cinnamon. Beat with electric mixer at high speed until stiff peaks form. Fold in melted chocolate pieces. Split pastries into 2 layers. Spread 12 rectangles with chocolate cream. Top with another rectangle. Spread with whipped cream, sliced strawberries and remaining rectangles. Serve immediately or cover and refrigerate up to 4 hours. Just before serving, drizzle with melted chocolate and sprinkle with confectioners' sugar.        *Makes 12 napoleons*

*Chocolate Mousse Napoleons
with Strawberries & Cream*

# Glazed Carrot Raisin Cupcakes

**Prep Time:** 10 minutes    **Cook Time:** 20 minutes
**Cool Time:** 20 minutes

- 1 package spice cake mix (about 18 ounces)
- 1 can (10¾ ounces) CAMPBELL'S HEALTHY REQUEST Condensed Tomato Soup
- ½ cup water
- 2 eggs
- 1 medium carrot, shredded (about ½ cup)
- ½ cup raisins
- 1 cup confectioners' sugar
- 3 tablespoons unsweetened apple juice

1. Preheat oven to 350°F. Place liners in 24 (2½-inch) muffin-pan cups. Set aside.

2. Mix cake mix, soup, water and eggs according to package directions. Fold in carrot and raisins. Spoon batter into cups, filling almost full.

3. Bake 20 minutes or until toothpick inserted in center comes out clean. Remove from pan and cool completely on wire rack.

4. Mix sugar and juice until smooth. Frost cupcakes.

*Makes 24 cupcakes*

**Nutritional Values per Serving:** Calories 124, Total Fat 2g, Saturated Fat 0g, Cholesterol 18mg, Sodium 182mg, Total Carbohydrate 24g, Protein 1g

*Glazed Carrot Raisin Cupcakes*

# Campbell's
# HOLIDAY TABLE TRADITIONS

## Green Bean Bake

**Prep Time:** 10 minutes      **Cook Time:** 30 minutes

1 can (10¾ ounces) CAMPBELL'S Condensed Cream
  of Mushroom Soup *or* 98% Fat Free Cream of
  Mushroom Soup
½ cup milk
1 teaspoon soy sauce
  Dash pepper
4 cups cooked cut green beans
1 can (2.8 ounces) French fried onions (1⅓ cups)

**1.** In 1½-quart casserole mix soup, milk, soy sauce, pepper, beans
and ½ *can* onions.

**2.** Bake at 350°F. for 25 minutes or until hot.

**3.** Stir. Sprinkle remaining onions over bean mixture. Bake 5
minutes more or until onions are golden.          *Serves 6*

**Tip:** Use 1 bag (16 to 20 ounces) frozen green beans, 2 packages
(9 ounces *each*) frozen green beans, 2 cans (about 16 ounces *each*)
green beans *or* about 1½ pounds fresh green beans for this recipe.

*Green Bean Bake*

# Holiday Turkey with Apple Pecan Stuffing

**Prep Time:** 30 minutes     **Cook Time:** 4½ to 5 hours
**Stand Time:** 10 minutes

¼ cup margarine *or* butter
2 stalks celery, chopped (about 1 cup)
1 large onion, chopped (about 1 cup)
2 cans (10½ ounces *each*) CAMPBELL'S Condensed Chicken Broth
1 bag (14 ounces) PEPPERIDGE FARM Cubed Herb Seasoned Stuffing
2 medium apples, cored and chopped (about 2 cups)
1 cup chopped pecans
1 (12- to 14-pound) turkey
Vegetable oil

1. In large saucepan over medium heat, heat margarine. Add celery and onion and cook until tender. Add broth. Heat to a boil. Remove from heat. Add stuffing, apples and pecans. Mix lightly.

2. Remove package of giblets and neck from turkey cavity. Rinse turkey with cold water and pat dry. Spoon stuffing lightly into neck and body cavities.* Fold loose skin over stuffing. Tie ends of drumsticks together. Place turkey, breast side up, on rack in shallow roasting pan. Brush with oil. Insert meat thermometer into thickest part of meat, not touching bone.

3. Roast at 325°F. for 4½ to 5 hours or until thermometer reads 180°F., drumstick moves easily, and center of stuffing reaches 165°F., basting occasionally with pan drippings. Begin checking doneness after 4 hours roasting time. Allow turkey to stand 10 minutes before slicing.                    *Serves 12 to 16*

*Bake any remaining stuffing in covered casserole with turkey 30 minutes or until hot.*

**Variation:** Omit apples and pecans.

Top to bottom: *Holiday Turkey with Apple Pecan Stuffing, Mom's Best Gravy (page 186) and Creamy Vegetable Medley (page 194)*

# Sausage Corn Bread Stuffing

**Prep Time:** 15 minutes      **Cook Time:** 25 minutes

  ¼ **pound bulk pork sausage**
1¼ **cups water**
  1 **tablespoon chopped fresh parsley** *or* **1 teaspoon dried parsley flakes**
  ½ **cup cooked whole kernel corn**
  ½ **cup shredded Cheddar cheese (2 ounces)**
  4 **cups PEPPERIDGE FARM Corn Bread Stuffing**

**1.** In large saucepan over medium-high heat, cook sausage until browned, stirring to separate meat. Pour off fat.

**2.** Stir in water, parsley, corn and cheese. Add stuffing. Mix lightly. Spoon into greased 1½-quart casserole.

**3.** Cover and bake at 350°F. for 25 minutes or until hot.

*Serves 6*

*Tip*

This stuffing bake brings a new flavor to the traditional holiday meal—and is easy enough for an everyday meal!

Top to bottom: *Sausage Corn Bread Stuffing and Scalloped Apple Bake (page 190)*

# Mom's Best Gravy

*(photo on cover and page 183)*
**Prep Time:** 5 minutes    **Cook Time:** 5 minutes

> 2 cans (10½ ounces *each*) FRANCO-AMERICAN
>     Turkey Gravy
> 6 tablespoons turkey pan drippings
> ¼ teaspoon pepper
> ⅛ teaspoon sage
>     Hot mashed potatoes

In small saucepan mix gravy, drippings, pepper and sage. Over medium heat, heat through. Serve over mashed potatoes.

*Makes 2½ cups*

**Mushroom-Herb Gravy:** Heat 6 tablespoons turkey drippings in large saucepan. Add 1 cup sliced mushrooms and ¼ teaspoon dried thyme leaves, crushed, and cook until mushrooms are tender. Add 2 cans (10½ ounces *each*) FRANCO-AMERICAN Turkey Gravy and heat through.

**Sautéed Garlic & Onion Gravy:** Heat 6 tablespoons turkey drippings in large saucepan. Add 1 cup chopped onion and 2 cloves garlic, minced, and cook until onion is tender. Add 2 cans (10½ ounces *each*) FRANCO-AMERICAN Turkey Gravy and heat through.

*Tip*

Didn't roast a turkey? Just substitute 2 tablespoons vegetable oil for the turkey drippings.

# Skinny Mashed Sweet Potatoes

*(photo on page 189)*
**Prep Time:** 10 minutes    **Cook Time:** 15 minutes

2 cans (14½ ounces *each*) SWANSON Chicken Broth
(3½ cups)
4 large sweet potatoes *or* yams, peeled and cut into
1-inch pieces (about 7½ cups)
Generous dash pepper
2 tablespoons packed brown sugar

1. In medium saucepan place broth and potatoes. Over high heat, heat to a boil. Reduce heat to medium. Cover and cook 10 minutes or until potatoes are tender. Drain, reserving broth.

2. Mash potatoes with *1¼ cups* broth and pepper. If needed, add additional broth until potatoes are desired consistency. Add brown sugar.                                    *Serves about 6*

**Note:** 1g fat per serving

**Skinny Mashed Potatoes:** Substitute 5 large potatoes, cut into 1-inch pieces (about 7½ cups) for sweet potatoes and omit brown sugar.
**Note:** ½g fat per serving (traditional mashed potato recipe: 8g fat per serving)

**Skinny Garlic Mashed Potatoes:** *(photo on page 197)* Substitute 2 cans (14½ ounces *each*) SWANSON Seasoned Chicken Broth with Roasted Garlic for Chicken Broth and 5 large potatoes, cut into 1-inch pieces, for sweet potatoes. Omit brown sugar.

# Bye Bye Butter Stuffing

**Prep Time:** 10 minutes    **Cook Time:** 15 minutes

> 1 can (14½ ounces) SWANSON Chicken Broth
>    (1¾ cups)
> Generous dash pepper
> 1 stalk celery, coarsely chopped (about ½ cup)
> 1 small onion, coarsely chopped (about ¼ cup)
> ½ cup sliced mushrooms (optional)
> 4 cups PEPPERIDGE FARM Herb Seasoned Stuffing

**1.** In medium saucepan mix broth, pepper, celery, onion and mushrooms. Over high heat, heat to a boil. Reduce heat to low. Cover and cook 5 minutes or until vegetables are tender.

**2.** Add stuffing. Mix lightly.     *Serves 5*

**Note:** 2g fat per serving (traditional stuffing recipe: 10g fat per serving)

# Roasted Turkey Pan Gravy

**Prep Time:** 5 minutes    **Cook Time:** 10 minutes

> 1 can (14½ ounces) SWANSON Chicken Broth
>    (1¾ cups)
> 3 tablespoons all-purpose flour

Remove turkey from roasting pan. Pour off fat. In roasting pan gradually mix broth into flour. Over medium heat, cook until mixture boils and thickens, stirring constantly.     *Serves about 4*

**Note:** ½g fat per serving (traditional turkey gravy recipe: 8g fat per serving)

Clockwise from top: *Skinny Mashed Sweet Potatoes (page 187), Roasted Turkey Pan Gravy and Bye Bye Butter Stuffing*

# Scalloped Apple Bake

*(photo on page 185)*

**Prep Time:** 25 minutes     **Cook Time:** 40 minutes

¼ cup margarine *or* butter, melted
¼ cup sugar
2 teaspoons grated orange peel
1 teaspoon ground cinnamon
1½ cups PEPPERIDGE FARM Corn Bread Stuffing
½ cup coarsely chopped pecans
1 can (16 ounces) whole berry cranberry sauce
⅓ cup orange juice *or* water
4 large cooking apples, cored and thinly sliced
(about 6 cups)

**1.** Lightly mix margarine, sugar, orange peel, cinnamon, stuffing and pecans and set aside.

**2.** Mix cranberry sauce, juice and apples. Add **half** the stuffing mixture. Mix lightly. Spoon into 8-inch square baking dish. Sprinkle remaining stuffing mixture over apple mixture.

**3.** Bake at 375°F. for 40 minutes or until apples are tender.

*Serves 6*

*Tip*

To melt margarine, remove wrapper and place in microwave-safe cup. Cover and microwave on HIGH 45 seconds.

# Vegetable Stuffing Bake

*(photo on page 193)*
**Prep Time:** 15 minutes     **Cook Time:** 35 minutes

4 cups PEPPERIDGE FARM Herb Seasoned Stuffing
2 tablespoons margarine *or* butter, melted
1 can (10¾ ounces) CAMPBELL'S Condensed Cream
     of Mushroom Soup *or* 98% Fat Free Cream of
     Mushroom Soup
½ cup sour cream
2 small zucchini, shredded (about 2 cups)
2 medium carrots, shredded (about 1 cup)
1 small onion, finely chopped (about ¼ cup)

**1.** Mix *1 cup* stuffing and margarine. Set aside.

**2.** Mix soup, sour cream, zucchini, carrots and onion. Add remaining stuffing. Mix lightly. Spoon into 1½-quart casserole. Sprinkle with reserved stuffing mixture.

**3.** Bake at 350°F. for 35 minutes or until hot.          *Serves 6*

# Creamed Onion Bake

**Prep Time:** 15 minutes     **Cook Time:** 30 minutes

> 4 tablespoons margarine *or* butter
> 1½ cups PEPPERIDGE FARM Corn Bread Stuffing
> 2 tablespoons chopped fresh parsley *or* 2 teaspoons dried parsley flakes
> 3 large onions, cut in half and sliced (about 3 cups)
> 1 can (10¾ ounces) CAMPBELL'S Condensed Cream of Mushroom Soup *or* 98% Fat Free Cream of Mushroom Soup
> ¼ cup milk
> 1 cup frozen peas
> 1 cup shredded Cheddar cheese (4 ounces)

**1.** Melt *2 tablespoons* margarine and mix with stuffing and parsley. Set aside.

**2.** In medium skillet over medium heat, heat remaining margarine. Add onions and cook until tender.

**3.** Stir in soup, milk and peas. Spoon into 2-quart shallow baking dish. Sprinkle cheese and stuffing mixture over soup mixture.

**4.** Bake at 350°F. for 30 minutes or until hot.          *Serves 6*

Top to bottom: *Vegetable Stuffing Bake (page 191) and Creamed Onion Bake*

# Creamy Vegetable Medley

*(photo on page 183)*

**Prep Time:** 15 minutes     **Cook Time:** 20 minutes

> 1 can (10¾ ounces) CAMPBELL'S Condensed Cream
>    of Celery Soup *or* 98% Fat Free Cream of Celery
>    Soup
> ½ cup milk
> 2 cups broccoli flowerets
> 2 medium carrots, sliced (about 1 cup)
> 1 cup cauliflower flowerets

**1.** In medium saucepan mix soup, milk, broccoli, carrots and
cauliflower. Over medium heat, heat to a boil.

**2.** Reduce heat to low. Cover and cook 15 minutes or until
vegetables are tender, stirring occasionally.          *Serves 6*

**Variation:** Omit milk. Substitute 1 bag (16 ounces) frozen vegetable
combination (broccoli, cauliflower, carrots) for fresh vegetables.

# Slim & Savory Vegetables

*(photo on page 213)*
**Prep Time:** 10 minutes    **Cook Time:** 10 minutes

**1 can (14½ ounces) SWANSON Chicken Broth
    (1¾ cups)
3 cups cut-up vegetables***

**1.** In medium saucepan mix broth and vegetables. Over medium-high heat, heat to a boil.

**2.** Reduce heat to low. Cover and cook 5 minutes or until vegetables are tender-crisp. Drain.

*Serves 4*

*\*Use a combination of broccoli flowerets, cauliflower flowerets, carrots and celery cut in 2-inch pieces.*

**Note:** 0g fat per serving (traditional steamed vegetable recipe with butter: 3g fat per serving)

**Garlic Slim & Savory Vegetables:** Substitute 1 can (14½ ounces) SWANSON Seasoned Chicken Broth with Roasted Garlic for Chicken Broth.

**Broth Seasoned Rice:** Reserve broth after vegetables are cooked (1½ cups). In medium saucepan over medium-high heat, heat broth to a boil. Add *½ cup* uncooked regular white rice. Cook according to package directions. *Serves 3*

*Tip*

Substitute 1 bag (16 ounces) frozen vegetable combination (broccoli, cauliflower, carrots) for fresh vegetables.

# COLD WEATHER COMFORTS

## Best Ever Meatloaf

**Prep Time:** 10 minutes     **Cook Time:** 1 hour 20 minutes

- 1 can (10¾ ounces) CAMPBELL'S Condensed Tomato Soup
- 2 pounds ground beef
- 1 pouch CAMPBELL'S Dry Onion Soup and Recipe Mix
- ½ cup dry bread crumbs
- 1 egg, beaten
- ¼ cup water

1. Mix *½ cup* tomato soup, beef, onion soup mix, bread crumbs and egg *thoroughly.* In baking pan shape *firmly* into 8- by 4-inch loaf.

2. Bake at 350°F. for 1¼ hours or until meat loaf is no longer pink (160°F.).

3. In small saucepan mix *2 tablespoons* drippings, remaining tomato soup and water. Heat through. Serve with meat loaf.

*Serves 8*

Top to bottom: *Skinny Garlic Mashed Potatoes (page 187) and Best Ever Meatloaf*

# Baked Macaroni & Cheese

**Prep Time:** 20 minutes      **Cook Time:** 20 minutes

> 1 can (10¾ ounces) CAMPBELL'S Condensed
>    Cheddar Cheese Soup
> ½ soup can milk
> ⅛ teaspoon pepper
> 2 cups hot cooked corkscrew *or* medium shell
>    macaroni (about 1½ cups uncooked)
> 1 tablespoon dry bread crumbs
> 2 teaspoons margarine *or* butter, melted

**1.** In 1-quart casserole mix soup, milk, pepper and macaroni.

**2.** Mix bread crumbs with margarine and sprinkle over macaroni mixture.

**3.** Bake at 400°F. for 20 minutes or until hot.          *Serves 4*

**To Double Recipe:** Double all ingredients, except increase margarine to 1 tablespoon, use 2-quart casserole and increase baking time to 25 minutes.

**Variation:** Substitute 2 cups hot cooked elbow macaroni (about 1 cup uncooked) for corkscrew *or* shell macaroni.

*Baked Macaroni & Cheese*

# No-Guilt Chicken Pot Pie

**Prep Time:** 10 minutes     **Cook Time:** 30 minutes

1 can (10¾ ounces) CAMPBELL'S Condensed 98%
   Fat Free Cream of Chicken Soup
1 package (about 9 ounces) frozen mixed
   vegetables, thawed (about 2 cups)
1 cup cubed cooked chicken
½ cup milk
1 egg
1 cup reduced fat all-purpose baking mix

1. Preheat oven to 400°F. In 9-inch pie plate mix soup, vegetables and chicken.

2. Mix milk, egg and baking mix. Pour over chicken mixture. Bake 30 minutes or until golden.                    *Serves 4*

**No-Guilt Turkey Pot Pie:** Substitute 1 cup cubed cooked turkey for chicken.

*Tip*

For a variation, substitute CAMPBELL'S Condensed Cream of Chicken Soup *or* Cream of Chicken Soup with Herbs.

*No-Guilt Chicken Pot Pie*

# Miracle Lasagna

**Prep Time:** 5 minutes    **Cook Time:** 1 hour
**Stand Time:** 5 minutes

1 jar (28 ounces) PREGO Traditional Pasta Sauce
6 *uncooked* lasagna noodles
1 container (15 ounces) ricotta cheese
8 ounces shredded mozzarella cheese (2 cups)
¼ cup grated Parmesan cheese

1. In 2-quart shallow baking dish (11- by 7-inch) spread *1 cup* pasta sauce. Top with *3 uncooked* lasagna noodles, ricotta cheese, *1 cup* mozzarella cheese, Parmesan cheese and *1 cup* pasta sauce. Top with remaining *3 uncooked* lasagna noodles and remaining pasta sauce. **Cover.**

2. Bake at 375°F. for 1 hour. Uncover and top with remaining mozzarella cheese. Let stand 5 minutes.                    *Serves 6*

**Meat or Mushroom Miracle Lasagna:** Use 3-quart shallow baking dish (13- by 9-inch). Proceed as in Step 1. Top Parmesan cheese with 1 pound ground beef *or* sausage, cooked and drained, *or* 2 cups sliced fresh mushrooms *or* 2 jars (4½ ounces *each*) sliced mushrooms, drained.

*Tip*

For a variation, substitute PREGO Pasta Sauce with Fresh Mushrooms *or* PREGO Italian Sausage & Garlic Pasta Sauce.

*Miracle Lasagna*

# Baked Ziti Supreme

**Prep Time:** 25 minutes    **Cook Time:** 30 minutes

   1 **pound ground beef**
   1 **medium onion, chopped (about ½ cup)**
   1 **jar (28 ounces) PREGO Pasta Sauce with Fresh**
      **Mushrooms**
1½ **cups shredded mozzarella cheese (6 ounces)**
   5 **cups hot cooked medium tube-shaped macaroni**
      **(about 3 cups uncooked)**
   ¼ **cup grated Parmesan cheese**

**1.** In large saucepan over medium-high heat, cook beef and onion until beef is browned, stirring to separate meat. Pour off fat.

**2.** Stir in pasta sauce, *1 cup* mozzarella cheese and macaroni. Spoon into 3-quart shallow baking dish. Sprinkle with remaining mozzarella cheese and Parmesan cheese. Bake at 350°F. for 30 minutes.

*Serves 6*

*Tip*

A salad of mixed greens and hot toasted garlic bread team perfectly with this quick and easy casserole.

*Baked Ziti Supreme*

# Beef & Mozzarella Bake

**Prep Time:** 15 minutes     **Cook Time:** 25 minutes

> 1 pound ground beef
> 1 can (11⅛ ounces) CAMPBELL'S Condensed Italian Tomato Soup
> 1 can (10¾ ounces) CAMPBELL'S Condensed Cream of Mushroom Soup
> 1¼ cups water
> 1 teaspoon dried basil leaves, crushed
> ¼ teaspoon pepper
> ⅛ teaspoon garlic powder *or* 1 clove garlic, minced
> 1½ cups shredded mozzarella cheese (6 ounces)
> 4 cups hot cooked medium shell macaroni (about 3 cups uncooked)

**1.** In medium skillet over medium-high heat, cook beef until browned, stirring to separate meat. Pour off fat.

**2.** Add soups, water, basil, pepper, garlic powder, *1 cup* cheese and macaroni. Spoon into 2-quart shallow baking dish. Bake at 400°F. for 20 minutes or until hot.

**3.** Stir. Sprinkle remaining cheese over beef mixture. Bake 5 minutes more or until cheese is melted.           *Serves 6*

**Variation:** Substitute 4 cups hot cooked elbow macaroni (about 2 cups uncooked) for shell macaroni.

*Beef & Mozzarella Bake*

# Beefy Macaroni Skillet

**Prep Time:** 10 minutes     **Cook Time:** 15 minutes

   1 **pound ground beef**
   1 **medium onion, chopped (about ½ cup)**
   1 **can (10¾ ounces) CAMPBELL'S Condensed Tomato Soup**
  ¼ **cup water**
   1 **tablespoon Worcestershire sauce**
  ½ **cup shredded Cheddar cheese (2 ounces)**
   2 **cups cooked corkscrew macaroni (about 1½ cups uncooked)**

**1.** In medium skillet over medium-high heat, cook beef and onion until beef is browned, stirring to separate meat. Pour off fat.

**2.** Add soup, water, Worcestershire, cheese and macaroni. Reduce heat to low and heat through.      *Serves 4*

**Variation:** Substitute 2 cups cooked elbow macaroni (about 1 cup uncooked) for corkscrew macaroni.

*Tip*

This one-skillet family-pleaser works perfectly as a busy weekday or casual weekend meal.

*Beefy Macaroni Skillet*

# Stroganoff-Style Chicken

**Prep Time:** 15 minutes    **Cook Time:** 25 minutes

2 tablespoons vegetable oil
1 pound skinless, boneless chicken breasts, cut into strips
2 cups sliced mushrooms (about 6 ounces)
1 medium onion, chopped (about ½ cup)
1 can (10¾ ounces) CAMPBELL'S HEALTHY REQUEST Condensed Cream of Chicken Soup
½ cup plain nonfat yogurt
¼ cup water
4 cups hot cooked medium egg noodles (about 3 cups uncooked), cooked without salt
Paprika

1. In medium skillet over medium-high heat, heat **half** the oil. Add chicken in 2 batches and cook until browned, stirring often. Set chicken aside.

2. Reduce heat to medium. Add remaining oil. Add mushrooms and onion and cook until tender.

3. Add soup, yogurt and water. Heat to a boil. Return chicken to pan and heat through. Serve over noodles. Sprinkle with paprika.

*Serves 4*

**Nutritional Values per Serving:** Calories 499, Total Fat 14g, Saturated Fat 3g, Cholesterol 132mg, Sodium 394mg, Total Carbohydrate 53g, Protein 38g

*Stroganoff-Style Chicken*

# Autumn Pork Chops

**Prep Time:** 5 minutes     **Cook Time:** 25 minutes

    1 tablespoon vegetable oil
    4 pork chops, ¾ inch thick (about 1½ pounds)
    1 can (10¾ ounces) CAMPBELL'S Condensed Cream
        of Celery Soup *or* 98% Fat Free Cream of Celery
        Soup
    ½ cup apple juice *or* water
    2 tablespoons spicy brown mustard
    1 tablespoon honey
      Generous dash pepper

**1.** In medium skillet over medium-high heat, heat oil. Add chops and cook 10 minutes or until browned. Set chops aside. Pour off fat.

**2.** Add soup, apple juice, mustard, honey and pepper. Heat to a boil. Return chops to pan. Reduce heat to low. Cover and cook 10 minutes or until chops are no longer pink.     *Serves 4*

*Tip*

You can store uncooked fresh pork tightly wrapped in butcher paper in the refrigerator up to four or five days. Freeze uncooked pork for up to one month.

Clockwise from left: *Scalloped Potato-Onion Bake (page 217), Slim & Savory Vegetables (page 195) and Autumn Pork Chop*

# Savory Chicken Stew

**Prep Time:** 15 minutes     **Cook Time:** 35 minutes

  1 tablespoon vegetable oil
  1 pound skinless, boneless chicken breasts, cut into
     1-inch pieces
  1 can (10¾ ounces) CAMPBELL'S Condensed Cream
     of Chicken & Broccoli Soup
  ½ cup milk
  ⅛ teaspoon pepper
  4 small red potatoes (about ¾ pound), cut into
     quarters
  2 medium carrots, sliced (about 1 cup)
  1 cup broccoli flowerets

**1.** In medium skillet over medium-high heat, heat oil. Add chicken in 2 batches and cook until browned, stirring often. Set chicken aside. Pour off fat.

**2.** Add soup, milk, pepper, potatoes, carrots and broccoli. Heat to a boil. Reduce heat to low. Cover and cook 15 minutes, stirring occasionally.

**3.** Return chicken to pan. Cover and cook 5 minutes or until chicken is no longer pink and vegetables are tender, stirring occasionally.

*Serves 4*

Top to bottom: *Homestyle Beef Stew (page 216) and Savory Chicken Stew*

# Homestyle Beef Stew

*(photo on page 215)*

**Prep Time:** 10 minutes     **Cook Time:** 2 hours 15 minutes

2 tablespoons all-purpose flour
⅛ teaspoon pepper
1 pound beef for stew, cut into 1-inch cubes
1 tablespoon vegetable oil
1 can (10½ ounces) CAMPBELL'S Condensed Beef Broth
½ cup water
½ teaspoon dried thyme leaves, crushed
1 bay leaf
3 medium carrots (about ½ pound), cut into 1-inch pieces
2 medium potatoes (about ½ pound), cut into quarters

1. Mix flour and pepper. Coat beef with flour mixture.

2. In Dutch oven over medium-high heat, heat oil. Add beef and cook until browned, stirring often. Set beef aside. Pour off fat.

3. Add broth, water, thyme and bay leaf. Heat to a boil. Return beef to pan. Reduce heat to low. Cover and cook 1½ hours.

4. Add carrots and potatoes. Cover and cook 30 minutes more or until beef is fork-tender, stirring occasionally. Discard bay leaf.

*Serves 4*

# Scalloped Potato-Onion Bake

*(photo on page 213)*

**Prep Time:** 15 minutes    **Cook Time:** 1 hour 15 minutes

    1 can (10¾ ounces) CAMPBELL'S Condensed Cream
        of Celery Soup *or* 98% Fat Free Cream of Celery
        Soup
    ½ cup milk
        Dash pepper
    4 medium potatoes (about 1¼ pounds), thinly sliced
    1 small onion, thinly sliced (about ¼ cup)
    1 tablespoon margarine *or* butter
        Paprika

1. Mix soup, milk and pepper. In 1½-quart casserole layer **half** the
   potatoes, onion and soup mixture. Repeat layers. Dot with
   margarine. Sprinkle with paprika.

2. Cover and bake at 400°F. for 1 hour. Uncover and bake 15 minutes
   more or until potatoes are tender.                    *Serves 6*

*Tip*

For a variation and dash of color, add ¼ cup chopped
fresh parsley in step 1.

# Skinny Potato Soup

**Prep Time:** 15 minutes      **Cook Time:** 30 minutes

1 can (14½ ounces) SWANSON Chicken Broth
    (1¾ cups)
⅛ teaspoon pepper
4 green onions, sliced (about ½ cup)
1 stalk celery, sliced (about ½ cup)
3 medium potatoes (about 1 pound), peeled and
    sliced ¼ inch thick
1½ cups milk

1. In medium saucepan mix broth, pepper, onions, celery and potatoes. Over high heat, heat to a boil. Reduce heat to low. Cover and cook 15 minutes or until vegetables are tender. Remove from heat.

2. In blender or food processor, place **half** the broth mixture and **¾ cup** milk. Cover and blend until smooth. Repeat with remaining broth mixture and remaining milk. Return to pan. Over medium heat, heat through.                          *Serves 5*

**Note:** 2g fat per serving (traditional vichyssoise recipe: 15g fat per serving)

*Tip*

In warm weather, serve Chilled Skinny Potato Soup.
After blending, pour soup into a serving bowl.
Refrigerate at least 2 hours.

Top to bottom: *Skinny Clam Chowder (page 221),*
*Quick Vegetable Soup (page 220)*
*and Skinny Potato Soup*

# Quick Vegetable Soup

*(photo on page 219)*
**Prep Time:** 10 minutes    **Cook Time:** 20 minutes

   2 cans (14½ ounces *each*) SWANSON Vegetable
       Broth
   ½ teaspoon dried basil leaves, crushed
   ¼ teaspoon garlic powder
   1 can (about 14½ ounces) whole peeled tomatoes,
       cut up
   1 package (about 9 ounces) frozen mixed vegetables
       (about 2 cups)
   1 cup *uncooked* corkscrew macaroni

In medium saucepan mix broth, basil, garlic powder, tomatoes and
vegetables. Over medium-high heat, heat to a boil. Stir in
macaroni. Reduce heat to medium. Cook 15 minutes or until
macaroni is done, stirring occasionally.                    *Serves 6*

**Note:** 1g fat per serving

*Tip*

Homemade soup in just 30 minutes? SWANSON Broth
makes it easy and delicious. For a variation, substitute
1 cup uncooked elbow macaroni for
corkscrew macaroni.

# Skinny Clam Chowder

*(photo on page 219)*

**Prep Time:** 15 minutes    **Cook Time:** 25 minutes

1 can (14½ ounces) SWANSON Natural Goodness™
    Chicken Broth
¼ teaspoon dried thyme leaves, crushed
⅛ teaspoon pepper
3 medium potatoes, peeled and cut into cubes
    (about 3 cups)
1 stalk celery, sliced (about ½ cup)
1 medium onion, chopped (about ½ cup)
1½ cups milk
2 tablespoons all-purpose flour
2 cans (6½ ounces *each*) minced clams

**1.** In medium saucepan mix broth, thyme, pepper, potatoes, celery
and onion. Over high heat, heat to a boil. Reduce heat to low.
Cover and cook 15 minutes or until vegetables are tender.

**2.** In bowl gradually mix milk into flour until smooth. Gradually add
to broth mixture. Add clams. Cook until mixture boils and
thickens, stirring constantly.                                    *Serves 7*

**Note:** 2g fat per serving (traditional New England clam chowder
recipe: 10g fat per serving)

# TURKEY TILL IT'S GONE

## Turkey Broccoli Alfredo

**Prep Time:** 10 minutes     **Cook Time:** 15 minutes

6 ounces *uncooked* fettuccine
1 cup fresh *or* frozen broccoli flowerets
1 can (10¾ ounces) CAMPBELL'S Condensed Cream of Mushroom Soup *or* 98% Fat Free Cream of Mushroom Soup
½ cup milk
½ cup grated Parmesan cheese
1 cup cubed cooked turkey
¼ teaspoon freshly ground pepper

**1.** Prepare fettuccine according to package directions. Add broccoli for last 4 minutes of cooking time. Drain.

**2.** In same pan mix soup, milk, cheese, turkey, pepper and fettuccine mixture and heat through, stirring occasionally.

*Serves 4*

**Variation:** Substitute 8 ounces uncooked spaghetti for fettuccine.

*Turkey Broccoli Alfredo*

# Turkey Stuffing Divan

**Prep Time:** 15 minutes     **Cook Time:** 30 minutes

     1¼ cups boiling water
      4 tablespoons margarine *or* butter, melted
      4 cups PEPPERIDGE FARM Herb Seasoned Stuffing
      2 cups cooked broccoli cuts
      2 cups cubed cooked turkey
      1 can (10¾ ounces) CAMPBELL'S Condensed Cream
          of Celery Soup *or* 98% Fat Free Cream of Celery
          Soup
      ½ cup milk
      1 cup shredded Cheddar cheese (4 ounces)

**1.** Mix water and margarine. Add stuffing. Mix lightly.

**2.** Spoon into 2-quart shallow baking dish. Arrange broccoli and turkey over stuffing. In small bowl mix soup, milk and **½ cup** cheese. Pour over broccoli and turkey. Sprinkle remaining cheese over soup mixture.

**3.** Bake at 350°F. for 30 minutes or until hot.          *Serves 6*

**Variation:** Substitute 1 can (10¾ ounces) CAMPBELL'S Condensed Cream of Chicken Soup **or** 98% Fat Free Cream of Chicken Soup for Cream of Celery Soup. Substitute 2 cups cubed cooked chicken for turkey.

*Tip*

For 2 cups cooked broccoli cuts use about 1 pound fresh broccoli, trimmed, cut into 1-inch pieces (about 2 cups) *or* 1 package (10 ounces) frozen broccoli cuts (2 cups).

*Turkey Stuffing Divan*

# Turkey Asparagus Gratin

**Prep Time:** 20 minutes     **Cook Time:** 30 minutes

> 1 can (10¾ ounces) CAMPBELL'S Condensed Cream
>   of Asparagus Soup
> ½ cup milk
> ¼ teaspoon onion powder
> ⅛ teaspoon pepper
> 3 cups hot cooked corkscrew macaroni (about
>   2½ cups uncooked)
> 1½ cups cubed cooked turkey *or* chicken
> 1½ cups cooked cut asparagus
> 1 cup shredded Cheddar *or* Swiss cheese (4 ounces)

**1.** In 2-quart casserole mix soup, milk, onion powder and pepper.
Stir in macaroni, turkey, asparagus and **½ cup** cheese.

**2.** Bake at 400°F. for 25 minutes or until hot.

**3.** Stir. Sprinkle remaining cheese over turkey mixture. Bake
5 minutes more or until cheese is melted.          *Serves 4*

*Tip*

For 1½ cups cooked cut asparagus, cook ¾ pound
fresh asparagus, trimmed and cut into 1-inch pieces **or**
1 package (about 9 ounces) frozen asparagus cuts.

*Turkey Asparagus Gratin*

# Turkey Primavera

**Prep Time:** 10 minutes     **Cook Time:** 20 minutes

1 can (10¾ ounces) CAMPBELL'S HEALTHY REQUEST
   Condensed Cream of Mushroom Soup
½ cup milk
3 tablespoons grated Parmesan cheese
¼ teaspoon garlic powder
1 bag (16 ounces) frozen vegetable combination
   (broccoli, cauliflower, carrots)
2 cups cubed cooked turkey *or* chicken
4 cups hot cooked spaghetti (about 8 ounces
   uncooked), cooked without salt

**1.** In medium saucepan mix soup, milk, cheese, garlic powder and
vegetables. Over medium heat, heat to a boil. Reduce heat to
low. Cover and cook 10 minutes or until vegetables are tender-
crisp, stirring occasionally.

**2.** Add turkey and heat through. Serve over spaghetti.

*Serves 4*

**Nutritional Values per Serving:** Calories 415, Total Fat 9g, Saturated Fat 3g,
Cholesterol 58mg, Sodium 466mg, Total Carbohydrate 54g, Protein 30g

No cooked turkey or chicken on hand? Substitute
2 (5-ounce) cans of SWANSON Premium Chunk
Chicken Breast or Chunk Chicken.

In this recipe, HEALTHY REQUEST creates a creamy
sauce without the fat and calories of butter and cream!

*Turkey Primavera*

# Country Turkey Casserole

**Prep Time:** 20 minutes     **Cook Time:** 25 minutes

1 can (10¾ ounces) CAMPBELL'S Condensed Cream of Celery Soup *or* 98% Fat Free Cream of Celery Soup
1 can (10¾ ounces) CAMPBELL'S Condensed Cream of Potato Soup
1 cup milk
¼ teaspoon dried thyme leaves, crushed
⅛ teaspoon pepper
4 cups cooked cut-up vegetables*
2 cups cubed cooked turkey *or* chicken
4 cups prepared PEPPERIDGE FARM Herb Seasoned Stuffing

**1.** In 3-quart shallow baking dish mix soups, milk, thyme, pepper, vegetables and turkey. Spoon stuffing over turkey mixture.

**2.** Bake at 400°F. for 25 minutes or until hot.          *Serves 5*

*Use a combination of green beans cut into 1-inch pieces and sliced carrots.*

*Tip*

For prepared stuffing, heat 1¼ cups water and 4 tablespoons margarine **or** butter to a boil. Remove from heat and add 4 cups PEPPERIDGE FARM Herb Seasoned Stuffing. Mix lightly.

*Country Turkey Casserole*

# Turkey Broccoli Twists

**Prep Time:** 10 minutes     **Cook Time:** 20 minutes

3 cups *uncooked* corkscrew macaroni
2 cups broccoli flowerets
2 medium carrots, sliced (about 1 cup)
1 can (10¾ ounces) CAMPBELL'S Condensed Cream
    of Broccoli Soup *or* 98% Fat Free Cream of
    Broccoli Soup
1 can (14½ ounces) SWANSON Chicken Broth
    (1¾ cups)
½ teaspoon garlic powder
⅛ teaspoon pepper
2 cups cubed cooked turkey
¼ cup grated Parmesan cheese

**1.** In large saucepan prepare macaroni according to package
directions, omitting salt. Add broccoli and carrots for last
5 minutes of cooking time. Drain.

**2.** In same pan mix soup, broth, garlic powder, pepper, turkey and
macaroni mixture. Over medium heat, heat through, stirring
occasionally. Sprinkle with cheese.                    *Serves 5*

*Turkey Broccoli Twists*

# Easy Turkey & Biscuits

**Prep Time:** 15 minutes     **Cook Time:** 30 minutes

1 can (10¾ ounces) CAMPBELL'S Condensed Cream
    of Celery Soup *or* 98% Fat Free Cream of Celery
    Soup
1 can (10¾ ounces) CAMPBELL'S Condensed Cream
    of Potato Soup
1 cup milk
¼ teaspoon dried thyme leaves, crushed
¼ teaspoon pepper
4 cups cooked cut-up vegetables*
2 cups cubed cooked turkey, chicken *or* ham
1 package (7½ *or* 10 ounces) refrigerated buttermilk
    biscuits (10 biscuits)

**1.** In 3-quart shallow baking dish mix soups, milk, thyme, pepper, vegetables and turkey.

**2.** Bake at 400°F. for 15 minutes or until hot.

**3.** Stir. Arrange biscuits over turkey mixture. Bake 15 minutes more or until biscuits are golden.                *Serves 5*

*\*Use a combination of broccoli flowerets, cauliflower flowerets and sliced carrots **or** broccoli flowerets and sliced carrots **or** broccoli flowerets, sliced carrots and peas.*

*Tip*

To microwave vegetables, in 2-quart shallow microwave-safe baking dish arrange vegetables and ¼ cup water. Cover. Microwave on HIGH 10 minutes.

*Easy Turkey & Biscuits*

# Zesty Turkey & Rice

**Prep Time:** 5 minutes    **Cook Time:** 30 minutes

   1 can (14½ ounces) SWANSON Chicken Broth
      (1¾ cups)
   1 teaspoon dried basil leaves, crushed
  ¼ teaspoon garlic powder
  ¼ teaspoon hot pepper sauce
   1 can (about 14½ ounces) stewed tomatoes
  ¾ cup *uncooked* regular long-grain white rice
   1 cup frozen peas
   2 cups cubed cooked turkey *or* chicken

**1.** In medium saucepan mix broth, basil, garlic powder, hot pepper sauce and tomatoes. Over medium-high heat, heat to a boil. Stir in rice. Reduce heat to low. Cover and cook 20 minutes.

**2.** Stir in peas and turkey. Cover and cook 5 minutes more or until rice is done and most of liquid is absorbed.      *Serves 4*

**Note:** 3g fat per serving

*Tip*

The "zesty" in this all-in-one dish comes from the hot
pepper sauce. If your tastes run to mild,
just add a dash.

*Zesty Turkey & Rice*

# Barbecued Turkey Pockets

**Prep Time:** 10 minutes     **Cook Time:** 15 minutes

> 1 can (10¾ ounces) CAMPBELL'S HEALTHY REQUEST
>   Condensed Tomato Soup
> ¼ cup water
> 2 tablespoons packed brown sugar
> 2 tablespoons vinegar
> 1 tablespoon Worcestershire sauce
> 1 pound thinly sliced roasted *or* deli turkey breast
> 3 pita breads (6-inch), cut in half, forming 2 pockets

**1.** In medium skillet mix soup, water, sugar, vinegar and Worcestershire. Over medium heat, heat to a boil. Reduce heat to low and cook 5 minutes.

**2.** Add turkey and heat through. Spoon ½ cup turkey mixture into each pita half.                     *Makes 6 sandwiches*

**Nutritional Values per Serving:** Calories 241, Total Fat 2g, Saturated Fat 0g, Cholesterol 63mg, Sodium 433mg, Total Carbohydrate 29g, Protein 26g

*Tip*

Serve these flavorful pockets with a tossed salad, fresh sliced tomatoes or fresh fruit.

In this recipe, the rich flavor of HEALTHY REQUEST soup substitutes for a higher-in-sodium barbecue sauce.

Top to bottom: *Barbecued Turkey Pocket and Hearty Turkey Vegetable Soup (page 240)*

# Hearty Turkey Vegetable Soup

*(photo on page 239)*

**Prep Time:** 10 minutes     **Cook Time:** 20 minutes

3 cans (14½ ounces *each*) SWANSON Chicken Broth
   (5¼ cups)
½ teaspoon dried thyme leaves, crushed
¼ teaspoon garlic powder *or* 2 cloves garlic, minced
2 cups frozen whole kernel corn
1 package (about 10 ounces) frozen cut green beans
   (about 2 cups)
1 cup cut-up canned tomatoes
1 stalk celery, chopped (about ½ cup)
2 cups cubed cooked turkey *or* chicken

**1.** In large saucepan mix broth, thyme, garlic powder, corn, beans, tomatoes and celery. Over medium-high heat, heat to a boil. Reduce heat to low. Cover and cook 5 minutes or until vegetables are tender.

**2.** Add turkey and heat through.                                   *Serves 6*

**Note:** 2g fat per serving

*Tip*

For 2 cups cubed cooked chicken, in medium
saucepan over medium heat, in 4 cups of
boiling water, cook 1 pound skinless, boneless
chicken breasts, cubed, 5 minutes or until chicken
is no longer pink.

# My Favorites

# *My Favorite Recipes*

**Favorite recipe:** _____

**Favorite recipe from:** _____

**Ingredients:** _____

_____

_____

_____

_____

_____

**Method:** _____

_____

_____

_____

_____

_____

_____

_____

_____

_____

_____

_____

# My Favorite Recipes

**Favorite recipe:** _____

**Favorite recipe from:** _____

**Ingredients:** _____

_____

_____

_____

_____

_____

**Method:** _____

_____

_____

_____

_____

_____

_____

_____

_____

_____

_____

_____

# My Favorite Recipes

**Favorite recipe:** _____

**Favorite recipe from:** _____

**Ingredients:** _____

_____

_____

_____

_____

_____

**Method:** _____

_____

_____

_____

_____

_____

_____

_____

_____

_____

# *My Favorite Recipes*

**Favorite recipe:** _____

**Favorite recipe from:** _____

**Ingredients:** _____

_____

_____

_____

_____

_____

**Method:** _____

_____

_____

_____

_____

_____

_____

_____

_____

_____

_____

# My Favorite Recipes

**Favorite recipe:** _____

**Favorite recipe from:** _____

**Ingredients:** _____

_____

_____

_____

_____

_____

**Method:** _____

_____

_____

_____

_____

_____

_____

_____

_____

_____

_____

_____

# *My Favorite Recipes*

**Favorite recipe:** _____

**Favorite recipe from:** _____

**Ingredients:** _____

_____

_____

_____

_____

_____

**Method:** _____

_____

_____

_____

_____

_____

_____

_____

_____

_____

_____

_____

# My Favorite Recipes

**Favorite recipe:** _____

**Favorite recipe from:** _____

**Ingredients:** _____

_____

_____

_____

_____

_____

_____

**Method:** _____

_____

_____

_____

_____

_____

_____

_____

_____

_____

_____

# My Favorite Recipes

**Favorite recipe:** _____

**Favorite recipe from:** _____

**Ingredients:** _____

_____

_____

_____

_____

_____

**Method:** _____

_____

_____

_____

_____

_____

_____

_____

_____

_____

_____

# My Favorite Recipes

**Favorite recipe:** _____

**Favorite recipe from:** _____

**Ingredients:** _____

_____

_____

_____

_____

_____

_____

**Method:** _____

_____

_____

_____

_____

_____

_____

_____

_____

_____

_____

# *My Favorite Recipes*

**Favorite recipe:** _____

**Favorite recipe from:** _____

**Ingredients:** _____

_____

_____

_____

_____

**Method:** _____

_____

_____

_____

_____

_____

_____

_____

_____

_____

# My Favorite Recipes

**Favorite recipe:** _____

**Favorite recipe from:** _____

**Ingredients:** _____

_____

_____

_____

_____

_____

**Method:** _____

_____

_____

_____

_____

_____

_____

_____

_____

_____

_____

# *My Favorite Recipes*

**Favorite recipe:** _____

**Favorite recipe from:** _____

**Ingredients:** _____

_____

_____

_____

_____

_____

**Method:** _____

_____

_____

_____

_____

_____

_____

_____

_____

_____

_____

_____

# My Favorite Recipes

**Favorite recipe:** _____

**Favorite recipe from:** _____

**Ingredients:** _____

_____

_____

_____

_____

_____

**Method:** _____

_____

_____

_____

_____

_____

_____

_____

_____

_____

_____

# My Favorite Recipes

**Favorite recipe:** _____

**Favorite recipe from:** _____

**Ingredients:** _____

_____

_____

_____

_____

_____

**Method:** _____

_____

_____

_____

_____

_____

_____

_____

_____

_____

_____

# My Favorite Recipes

**Favorite recipe:** _____

**Favorite recipe from:** _____

**Ingredients:** _____

_____

_____

_____

_____

_____

**Method:** _____

_____

_____

_____

_____

_____

_____

_____

_____

_____

_____

# My Favorite Recipes

**Favorite recipe:** _____

**Favorite recipe from:** _____

**Ingredients:** _____
_____
_____
_____
_____
_____

**Method:** _____
_____
_____
_____
_____
_____
_____
_____
_____
_____
_____
_____

# My Favorite Recipes

**Favorite recipe:** _____

**Favorite recipe from:** _____

**Ingredients:** _____

_____

_____

_____

_____

_____

**Method:** _____

_____

_____

_____

_____

_____

_____

_____

_____

_____

_____

# *My Favorite Recipes*

**Favorite recipe:** _____

**Favorite recipe from:** _____

**Ingredients:** _____

_____

_____

_____

_____

_____

**Method:** _____

_____

_____

_____

_____

_____

_____

_____

_____

_____

_____

_____

# *My Favorite Recipes*

**Favorite recipe:** _____

**Favorite recipe from:** _____

**Ingredients:** _____

_____

_____

_____

_____

_____

**Method:** _____

_____

_____

_____

_____

_____

_____

_____

_____

_____

_____

# *My Favorite Recipes*

**Favorite recipe:** _____

**Favorite recipe from:** _____

**Ingredients:** _____

_____

_____

_____

_____

_____

**Method:** _____

_____

_____

_____

_____

_____

_____

_____

_____

_____

_____

# *My Favorite Dinner Party*

**Date:** _____

**Occasion:** _____

_____

**Guests:** _____

_____

_____

_____

_____

**Menu:** _____

_____

_____

_____

_____

_____

_____

_____

_____

_____

_____

_____

# My Favorite Dinner Party

**Date:** _____

**Occasion:** _____

_____

**Guests:** _____

_____

_____

_____

_____

**Menu:** _____

_____

_____

_____

_____

_____

_____

_____

_____

_____

# *My Favorite Dinner Party*

**Date:** _____

**Occasion:** _____

_____

**Guests:** _____

_____

_____

_____

_____

**Menu:** _____

_____

_____

_____

_____

_____

_____

_____

_____

_____

_____

# My Favorite Dinner Party

**Date:** _____

**Occasion:** _____
_____

**Guests:** _____
_____
_____
_____
_____

**Menu:** _____
_____
_____
_____
_____
_____
_____
_____
_____
_____

## My Favorite Brunch

**Date:** _____

**Occasion:** _____
_____

**Guests:** _____
_____
_____
_____
_____

**Menu:** _____
_____
_____
_____
_____
_____
_____
_____
_____
_____
_____

## *My Favorite Brunch*

**Date:** _____

**Occasion:** _____

_____

**Guests:** _____

_____

_____

_____

_____

**Menu:** _____

_____

_____

_____

_____

_____

_____

_____

_____

_____

_____

_____

# *My Favorite Brunch*

**Date:** _____

**Occasion:** _____

_____

**Guests:** _____

_____

_____

_____

_____

**Menu:** _____

_____

_____

_____

_____

_____

_____

_____

_____

_____

_____

_____

# My Favorite Brunch

**Date:** _____

**Occasion:** _____

_____

**Guests:** _____

_____

_____

_____

_____

**Menu:** _____

_____

_____

_____

_____

_____

_____

_____

_____

_____

_____

_____

_____

# My Favorite Food Gifts

**Friend:** _____

**Date:** _____

**Food Gift:** _____

_____

_____

_____

**Friend:** _____

**Date:** _____

**Food Gift:** _____

_____

_____

_____

**Friend:** _____

**Date:** _____

**Food Gift:** _____

_____

_____

_____

# *My Favorite Food Gifts*

**Friend:** _____

**Date:** _____

**Food Gift:** _____

_____

_____

_____


**Friend:** _____

**Date:** _____

**Food Gift:** _____

_____

_____

_____


**Friend:** _____

**Date:** _____

**Food Gift:** _____

_____

_____

_____

# *My Favorite Friends*

**Friend:** _____

**Favorite foods:** _____
_____

**Don't serve:** _____
_____
_____

**Friend:** _____

**Favorite foods:** _____
_____

**Don't serve:** _____
_____
_____

**Friend:** _____

**Favorite foods:** _____
_____

**Don't serve:** _____
_____
_____

# My Favorite Friends

**Friend:** _____

**Favorite foods:** _____

_____

**Don't serve:** _____

_____

_____

**Friend:** _____

**Favorite foods:** _____

_____

**Don't serve:** _____

_____

_____

**Friend:** _____

**Favorite foods:** _____

_____

**Don't serve:** _____

_____

_____

# Hints, Tips & Index

Hints, Tips & Index

# Quick Cooking Tips

To avoid last minute stress, take a few minutes to plan family menus a week in advance. Remember that *Campbell's* cookbooks are a great resource for quick homemade meal ideas!

Save time by being prepared! Read through a recipe completely and assemble all ingredients before you begin cooking.

Cut down on shopping time—keep CAMPBELL'S Condensed Soups on hand. You can make easy and delicious everyday meals with ingredients right from the pantry!

Feed the kids quickly with CAMPBELL'S Cheddar Cheese Soup! Just mix it with cooked chicken and PACE Salsa for a great quesadilla filling, or pour over baked potatoes or nachos.

No more need to chop mushrooms or garlic! Just use CAMPBELL'S Cream of Mushroom with Roasted Garlic Soup to instantly add delicious flavor to meat, poultry, pasta and rice.

Stir your favorite CAMPBELL'S Condensed Soup into cooked instant rice for a savory side dish in no time!

Double a recipe and freeze or refrigerate half for an instant meal later in the week.

When a recipe will be served over pasta or rice, save time by heating the cooking water while you're preparing the recipe. It'll be ready when you are!

If a recipe calls for cooked pasta and vegetables, save time by cooking them together! Add the vegetables partway through the cooking time.

If a recipe calls for cooked pasta and time is short, use faster cooking pastas, such as angel hair and spaghetti.

When a recipe calls for chicken strips, don't spend time slicing chicken breasts—buy chicken tenders instead.

For pre-cooked chicken, substitute a 5-ounce can of SWANSON Premium Chicken Breast or Chunk Chicken for ¾ to 1 cup cooked chicken.

Salted water takes longer to boil. To save time, don't salt water until after it is boiling.

To defrost meat quickly and safely use your microwave! (Be sure to follow the manufacturer's instructions for defrosting.)

To quick-thaw frozen vegetables, remove from the packaging and place in a microwave-safe bowl. Cover with waxed paper and microwave on HIGH 2 to 3 minutes, breaking apart with a fork every 30 seconds until easily separated but not cooked.

For side dishes and mix-ins, keep frozen vegetables on hand instead of fresh—they cook faster and keep longer!

No time to chop fresh produce? Buy bags of pre-cut vegetables—they work great in many recipes!

Save on cleanup time by portioning food right from the pot onto dinner plates. Call it restaurant-style!

Save time by preparing your casserole in a baking dish that doubles as a serving dish—less cleanup!

Freeze make-ahead dishes in freezer/microwave-safe containers for speedy reheating.

Freeze leftovers in flat containers rather than deep ones. They will defrost faster.

### Casserole Cookware

Casserole cookware comes in a variety of shapes, sizes and materials that fall into 2 general descriptions. They can be either deep, round containers with handles and tight-fitting lids or square and rectangular baking dishes. Casseroles are made out of glass, ceramic or metal. When preparing a casserole, it's important to bake the casserole in the proper size dish so that the ingredients cook evenly in the time specified.

### Size Unknown?

If the size of the casserole or baking dish isn't marked on the bottom of the dish, it can be measured to determine the size.

• Round and oval casseroles are measured by volume, not inches, and are always listed by quart capacity. Fill a measuring cup with water and pour it into an empty casserole. Repeat until the casserole is filled with water, keeping track of the amount of water added. The amount of water is equivalent to the size of the dish.

• Square and rectangular baking dishes are usually measured in inches. If the dimensions aren't marked on the bottom of a square or rectangular baking dish, use a ruler to measure on top from the inside of one edge to the inside of the opposite edge.

### Helpful Preparation Techniques

Some of the recipes call for advance preparations, such as cooked chicken or pasta. In order to ensure success when following and preparing the recipes, here are several preparation tips and techniques.

### • Tips for Cooking Pasta

For every pound of pasta, bring 4 to 6 quarts of water to a rolling boil. Gradually add pasta, allowing water to return to a boil. Stir frequently to prevent the pasta from sticking together.

Pasta is finished cooking when it is tender but still firm to the bite, or al dente. The pasta continues to cook when the casserole is placed in the oven so it is important that the pasta be slightly undercooked. Otherwise, the more the pasta cooks, the softer it becomes and, eventually, it will fall apart.

Immediately drain pasta to prevent overcooking. For best results, combine pasta with other ingredients immediately after draining.

## • Tips for Cooking Rice

The different types of rice require different amounts of water and cooking times. Follow the package instructions for the best results.

Measure the amount of water specified on the package and pour into a medium saucepan. Bring to a boil over medium-high heat. Slowly add rice and return to a boil. Reduce heat to low. Cover and simmer for the time specified on the package or until the rice is tender and most of the water has been absorbed.

To test the rice for doneness, bite into a grain or squeeze a grain between your thumb and index finger. The rice is done when it is tender and the center is not hard.

## Top It Off!

Buttery, golden brown bread crumbs are a popular choice when it comes to topping a casserole. Making your own bread crumbs is a great way to use up a leftover loaf of bread. To make bread crumbs, preheat oven to 300°F. Place a single layer of bread slices on a baking sheet and bake 5 to 8 minutes or until completely dry and lightly browned. Cool completely. Process in food processor or crumble in resealable plastic food storage bag until very fine. For additional flavor, season with salt, pepper and a small amount of dried herbs, ground spices or grated cheese as desired. Generally, 1 slice of bread equals ⅓ cup bread crumbs.

### The Basics
• As with conventional cooking recipes, slow cooker recipe time ranges are provided to account for variables such as temperature of ingredients before cooking, how full the slow cooker is and even altitude. Once you become familiar with your slow cooker you'll have a good idea which end of the time range to use.

• Manufacturers recommend that slow cookers should be one-half to three-quarters full for best results.

• Keep a lid on it! The slow cooker can take as long as twenty minutes to regain the heat lost when the cover is removed. If the recipe calls for stirring or checking the dish near the end of the cooking time, replace the lid as quickly as you can.

• To clean your slow cooker, follow the manufacturer's instructions. To make cleanup even easier, spray with nonstick cooking spray before adding food.

• Always taste the finished dish before serving and adjust seasonings to your preference. Consider adding a dash of any of the following: salt, pepper, seasoned salt, seasoned herb blends, lemon juice, soy sauce, Worcestershire sauce, flavored vinegar, freshly ground pepper or minced fresh herbs.

### TIPS & TECHNIQUES

### Adapting Recipes
If you'd like to adapt your own favorite recipe to a slow cooker, you'll need to follow a few guidelines. First, try to find a similar recipe in this publication or your manufacturer's guide. Note the cooking times, liquid, quantity and size of meat and vegetable pieces. Because the slow cooker captures moisture, you will want to reduce the amount of liquid, often by as much as half. Add dairy products toward the end of the cooking time so they do not curdle.

# Slow Cooker Tips

### Selecting the Right Meat

A good tip to keep in mind while shopping is that you can, and in fact should, use tougher, inexpensive cuts of meat. Top-quality cuts, such as loin chops or filet mignon, fall apart during long cooking periods. Keep those for roasting, broiling or grilling and save money when you use your slow cooker. You will be amazed to find even the toughest cuts come out fork-tender and flavorful.

### Reducing Fat

The slow cooker can help you make meals lower in fat because you won't be cooking in fat as you do when you stir-fry and sauté. And tougher cuts of meat have less fat than prime cuts. If you do use fatty cuts, such as ribs, brown them first on top of the range to cook excess fat.

### Cutting Vegetables

Vegetables often take longer to cook than meats. Cut vegetables into small, thin pieces and place them on the bottom or near the sides of the slow cooker. Pay careful attention to the recipe instructions in order to cut vegetables to the proper size.

### Food Safety Tips

If you do any advance preparation, such as trimming meat or cutting vegetables, make sure you keep the food covered and refrigerated until you're ready to start cooking. Store uncooked meats and vegetables separately. If you are preparing meat, poultry or fish, remember to wash your cutting board, utensils and hands before touching other foods.

Once your dish is cooked, don't keep it in the slow cooker too long. Foods need to be kept cooler than 40°F or hotter than 140°F to avoid the growth of harmful bacteria. Remove food to a clean container and cover and refrigerate as soon as possible. Do not reheat leftovers in the slow cooker. Use a microwave oven, the range-top or the oven for reheating.

# Metric Conversion Chart

## VOLUME MEASUREMENTS (dry)

⅛ teaspoon = 0.5 mL
¼ teaspoon = 1 mL
½ teaspoon = 2 mL
¾ teaspoon = 4 mL
1 teaspoon = 5 mL
1 tablespoon = 15 mL
2 tablespoons = 30 mL
¼ cup = 60 mL
⅓ cup = 75 mL
½ cup = 125 mL
⅔ cup = 150 mL
¾ cup = 175 mL
1 cup = 250 mL
2 cups = 1 pint = 500 mL
3 cups = 750 mL
4 cups = 1 quart = 1 L

## VOLUME MEASUREMENTS (fluid)

1 fluid ounce (2 tablespoons) = 30 mL
4 fluid ounces (½ cup) = 125 mL
8 fluid ounces (1 cup) = 250 mL
12 fluid ounces (1½ cups) = 375 mL
16 fluid ounces (2 cups) = 500 mL

## WEIGHTS (mass)

½ ounce = 15 g
1 ounce = 30 g
3 ounces = 90 g
4 ounces = 120 g
8 ounces = 225 g
10 ounces = 285 g
12 ounces = 360 g
16 ounces = 1 pound = 450 g

## DIMENSIONS

1/16 inch = 2 mm
⅛ inch = 3 mm
¼ inch = 6 mm
½ inch = 1.5 cm
¾ inch = 2 cm
1 inch = 2.5 cm

## OVEN TEMPERATURES

250°F = 120°C
275°F = 140°C
300°F = 150°C
325°F = 160°C
350°F = 180°C
375°F = 190°C
400°F = 200°C
425°F = 220°C
450°F = 230°C

## BAKING PAN SIZES

| Utensil | Size in Inches/Quarts | Metric Volume | Size in Centimeters |
|---|---|---|---|
| Baking or Cake Pan (square or rectangular) | 8×8×2 | 2 L | 20×20×5 |
| | 9×9×2 | 2.5 L | 23×23×5 |
| | 12×8×2 | 3 L | 30×20×5 |
| | 13×9×2 | 3.5 L | 33×23×5 |
| Loaf Pan | 8×4×3 | 1.5 L | 20×10×7 |
| | 9×5×3 | 2 L | 23×13×7 |
| Round Layer Cake Pan | 8×1½ | 1.2 L | 20×4 |
| | 9×1½ | 1.5 L | 23×4 |
| Pie Plate | 8×1¼ | 750 mL | 20×3 |
| | 9×1¼ | 1 L | 23×3 |
| Baking Dish or Casserole | 1 quart | 1 L | — |
| | 1½ quart | 1.5 L | — |
| | 2 quart | 2 L | — |

# Recipe Index

# Recipe Index

# Recipe Index

# Recipe Index

# Recipe Index

# Recipe Index

# Product Index

# *Product Index*

# Product Index